"Author Sharla Goettl delivers a thoughtful, in-depth approach to creating a spiritual safe haven of our homes. With poignant personal stories and insights from the prophet Nephi and his family, Goettl's wisdom sheds new light on how to utilize the Spirit and keep our hearts open in our parenting. Studying this tender topic is well worth our time as we strive to create a strong foundation of love and peace in our homes while working together to exemplify the Savior."

—HEATHER B. MOORE, Author of *The Divinity of Women*

"Sharla Goettl's inspiring and thought-provoking book approaches the topic of teaching and preparing youth in a fresh and powerful way, one completely new to me. By examining Nephi's life and determining the qualities he exhibited in his early years, Sister Goettl helps readers see how they can prepare today's youth with the inspiration and ability to "go and do" as Nephi did. Her practical method made me wish I'd had this book as I raised my children—but now, as a grandmother, I have gleaned much that will help me be a positive influence in the lives of my grandchildren as I support their parents in raising a righteous generation prepared to meet the Savior."

—KATHRYN JENKINS OVESON, Extensive Author and
Former Managing Editor of Covenant Communications

"Every parent wants their children to grow up to be all Heavenly Father wants them to be. As a parent with four children (three of them teens), it is a challenge to know how to raise spiritually resilient children in such a difficult time in the world. Sharla Goettl's book, *Spiritual Resilience: Leading Our Youth to Go and Do*, is a great resource. Sharla shares insights from her own experience as a parent and youth leader, coupled with lessons learned from Nephi and his family in the Book of Mormon. In a time when intentional parenting is a necessity, Sharla's book provides thought-provoking insights and questions that can be a great help in parenting today's youth."

—BRIAN HOWARD, Host of *Latter-day Profiles* on BYUtv

Spiritual

RESILIENCE

Still shot of Nephi praying by Book of Mormon Video Production © By Intellectual Reserve, Inc. Courtesy of The Church of Jesus Christ of Latter-day Saints. Used by permission.

Spiritual
RESILIENCE

LEADING OUR YOUTH TO
GO AND DO

SHARLA GOETTL

CASTORAMERA PUBLISHING
Newberg, Oregon

Editorial work by Eschler Editing
Cover design by Erin Seaward-Hiatt
Interior print design and layout by Erin Seaward-Hiatt
Cover photograph by Carly Jane Thunell

Production services facilitated by Scrivener Books

Published by CastorAmera Publishing
Printed in the United States
2043 NE Chehalem Drive,
Newberg, OR 97132

ISBN   978-1-7363496-2-5

This book is dedicated to the young people in my life,
especially my daughters,
who have taught me and will continue to teach me
the lessons I need to learn.

"I will do right. As He dictates, so I will perform."

—BRIGHAM YOUNG, upon being sustained as President of The Church of Jesus Christ of Latter-day Saints[1]

Council Bluffs, Iowa
December 27, 1847

Table of Contents

Preface

WE ARE PART OF A VERY REAL, very powerful, very compassionate divine family. I love my Heavenly Parents for knowing what I would need and for providing it through the plan of salvation. I love my brother Jesus Christ because He has fulfilled His promise to replace my fears with peace through His covenants. I love the Holy Ghost for wanting to help me continually repent and guide me back to our true home.

My Savior has taught me not to fear. From a young age, He promised me I did not need to fear loneliness because I was baptized into a church fellowship. I now know I do not need to fear inadequacy because I can repent—again and again. I do not need to fear worthlessness because of the destiny described during my temple ordinances. I do not need to fear death because of the knowledge provided during my endowment. I do not need to fear isolation because of the sealing of my family. I do not need to fear losing my way because the Holy Ghost, my prophet, and the scriptures guide my steps.

Christ has promised that we do not need to be afraid of what lies ahead. Instead, we should acknowledge the consequences of our actions as Latter-day Saints, as members of Jesus Christ's own Church, and as parents of Christ's future leaders. Christ is asking us to be braver, more confident, and to go and do those things we are prompted to do. He knows the future will require a firmer faith. He is asking us to be more *spiritually resilient.*

My current calling in The Church of Jesus Christ of Latter-day Saints is to help the rising generation be better prepared for the role only they can play. This book is written to adults rather than to the youth because acquiring spiritual resilience is a deep process that requires life-size examples. Youth need to see the daily implications of our choices to understand what spiritual resilience means in action. As the adults leading God's future heroes, we must better exemplify a humility that feels gratitude for commandments and repentance, a faith that focuses on what we know rather than what we do not, a motivation to implement the direction we are given by God, and a fuller recognition of His interaction.

By design, many questions are addressed to you throughout this book. Following each chapter, space is given for your answers. I encourage you to prayerfully invite the Holy Ghost into this learning process. Only the Holy Ghost truly knows the answers that are right for your family. Therefore, we all need to be asking more questions and acknowledging the responses from the Holy Ghost. I have offered questions to help you pinpoint effective opportunities for your growth as well as for the growth of the children around you.

To begin this process, what do you feel God is asking you to do first? It can feel big, like an urgent change in direction. Or it can be a subtle, small adjustment needed in this moment. Both can come from the Holy Ghost, and both are effective at bringing people toward progress. It helps to write your answers down, so space has been provided to do so.

I want you to learn what I have learned from Nephi, but not in a way that makes you feel inadequate or stretched thin. Striving to better yourself should be personal, but, more specifically, it should be personally manageable. Do what you are prompted to do; nothing more or less will be as effective.

I focus only on the earliest chapters of 1 Nephi within The Book of Mormon—the period during which he is still a youth—for insight on how to help our youth. The principles in this book lay out the building blocks of Nephi's own testimony, especially his declaration "I will go and do," as found in 1 Nephi 3:7.

At the beginning of this book, you will find a chapter summary to help you quickly find those sections that feel most applicable right now.

You can make the learning process relevant by applying the principles we'll discuss to your situation. Mark up this book—the more, the better! Highlight passages you want to remember and ponder. Cross out parts that aren't the right fit, but explain why. Write down your insights, memorable experiences, personal examples, and layers of questions. Especially write the answers you receive from the Holy Ghost. Doing so will ensure that the time you spend reading and studying is relevant to you. Recognize that the Holy Ghost is often present in your thoughts; document His interactions with you and follow the process He leads you through.

We have little time in this busy world. Go and do! Make it relevant and make it matter!

> With appreciation for all you are doing
> and encouragement in all you want to do,
>
> SHARLA GOETTL

Chapter 1

I, NEPHI

How Did Nephi Do What He Did?

"But behold, I, Nephi, will show unto you that the tender mercies of the Lord are over all those whom he hath chosen, because of their faith, to make them mighty even unto the power of deliverance."

—1 NEPHI 1:20

SPIRIT-LED, RESILIENT, AND WISE: these are the qualities needed to serve in the Lord's battalion. The children of today have more access to gospel knowledge than in any other dispensation. They are more connected with their fellow followers of Christ than in any previous generation. They are charged to stay true to Christ as He leads them forward on His chosen path. For all these reasons, they have an unprecedented capacity to be mighty and powerful, destined to influence an ever-increasing portion of God's children. Therefore, their exemplars, teachers, and parents must also be wise, resilient, and Spirit-led.

The loss of faith among our youth is one of the most significant problems we face as a Church today—not because of the numerical loss of membership but because of the loss of their potential strength. When youth lose their testimonies, we lose the unique perspectives they offer when it comes to solutions and insights we may not currently see.

In his June 2018 address entitled "Hope of Israel," President Russell M. Nelson called the youth of our day to speak more boldly, act more intentionally, and ponder more deeply as they accept their role in gathering Israel and building the kingdom of God.[2] In April 2020, he wrote, "Why do we need such resilient faith? Because difficult days are ahead."[3]

When I heard this prophetic direction, my thoughts immediately went to the youth in my life and what I might be able to do to help and encourage them. How could I support an increase in their strength? What could I do to retain their sense of purpose and divine worth? How could I better help prepare them spiritually for a future I couldn't predict?

As a stake Young Women president, decade-long youth leader, and parent of three teenagers, I felt an urgent responsibility to find the answers to these questions.

Turning to the scriptures, I came to realize that we have been given more scriptural insight into Nephi's early life and family dynamics than that of any other ancient prophet. The fact that we first meet Nephi in his teenage years and are given a detailed account of his long journey toward discipleship cannot be a coincidence. That his story was placed at the beginning of the Book of Mormon, where we would read it repeatedly, was also not a coincidence.

In the first chapters of the Book of Mormon, we learn of Nephi, his parents, his brothers, and the struggles each faced. They tried to obey

God, rely on their prophet, and trust in a divinely arranged process despite their varying degrees of spiritual resilience. Can we not relate to such a family while trying to determine what is right for us? What about a ward family that is not always united but that is learning the gospel and trying to act on it while hoping for what Christ promises us?

What can we learn from Nephi that can be useful for us today? Nephi founded a nation, preserved a culture, and expounded the gospel to generations of his family. Surely, he had some experience in developing spiritual resilience. What principles helped him get started?

Nephi was able to leave his home and all that was familiar to him. He faced physical violence, betrayal, exposure to extreme elements, and nearly losing his life. He built a sea-worthy ship of "curious workmanship" (1 Nephi 18:1) despite his inexperience and limited resources. He placed his entire family in it, trusting in his abilities and the Lord's power enough to set sail across an ocean. Nephi had an understanding that the Lord had prepared a special place for his family, but he had no concept of how to get there or even how long it would take.

Nephi responded to his hardship in a way I wish I could—the way I hope my children will respond to hardship someday. Nephi kept the Lord's direction at the front of his mind, acting with determination in any way available to him. He trusted that the difficulties with his brothers, his lack of resources, and his own inadequacies would be solved in the Lord's way. He focused on what he could do; everything else he placed in the Lord's hands.

Nephi was asked to be increasingly faithful and to act on his faith despite the unknown. Our children are being asked to go and do the same—and at the same age as Nephi when he showed us the example of how to go and do. Just like Nephi, our youth are being asked to build their ships of faith.

Are we as parents not also asked to sacrifice our time and efforts to build more spiritually minded homes? Nephi was led by Christ through the details of his task. Our children also need to know they can be capable builders under the tutelage of Christ. Don't we adults need this reassurance as well? What doubts do you need to place in the Lord's hands while you first focus on the direction you have been given?

Where did Nephi get the spiritual resilience sufficient to do what he did? As a *teenager*, how did Nephi develop one of the strongest testimonies of which we know? Can the story of Nephi show us what we need to better support the youth of Christ's Church? My study of the prophet Nephi has answered many of my questions. I can say with certainty that his story is a powerful guide that can help us on our own spiritual journey as well as provide ideas on how to help our youth.

I've learned that spiritual resilience is what helps us consistently turn to our Savior while facing the weight of struggle, doubt, and sin. Each time we put our trust in Christ we will find that our reliance on Him is justified. He is lifting us, supporting us, and teaching us in personally relevant ways, line upon line. He is preparing us for greater spiritual reach by adding layers on top of our steadfast and immovable foundation. He will provide the knowledge how we need it, when we need it, when we ask for it, and when we take the steps to be worthy to receive it.

Nephi shows us the extent to which we can fully trust in our Savior and rely on Him. Nephi has taught me what spiritual resilience is and how to get it. Therefore, let's work on it together!

Nephi taught that the Holy Ghost is a real, active part of our lives. The often-quoted warning President Nelson gave in April 2018 emphasizes the need for spiritual guidance: "In coming days, it will not be possible to survive spiritually without the guiding, directing, comforting, and constant influence of the Holy Ghost."[4] And communication with the Holy Ghost is required not just to survive, but to thrive. His authority can guide our implementation of the commandments. Nephi demonstrates how our path toward incremental improvement can be led only by the Spirit.

Spiritual resilience is faith paired with unwavering action. Nephi's example can help us know where to start and where to improve. These chapters will help you define the building blocks of spiritual resilience and know how to apply them so that they eventually inspire your choices. Only through *your actions* can these building blocks be effectively taught to those within your circle of influence.

Our daily reactions, interactions, and intentions are all colored by the shades of our faith. Each of these choices communicates something of our faith to those who know us best. The scale and depth of the example—both good and bad—I set for my own children is overwhelming to me. My actions reveal my real character in a way that cannot be bleached out.

If our teachings are not backed by our actions, our teachings will always be questioned. However, our actions will always be full of mistakes. Therefore, our sincere efforts to make progress must be made clear. We must allow our *development* of spiritual resilience and our *teaching* of spiritual resilience to happen at the same time! Doing so will lead to more confidence, even in the midst of the negative attitudes, life changes, limitations, habits, and mistakes we all are striving to overcome. We will be better able to manage the daily struggles of life because we have an eternal perspective. We can more fully trust Christ and be trusted by Him. When we do what we must to build spiritual resilience we will have less fear of our inability and more confidence in stepping forward.

In the recent past we have begun a spiritual journey through home-taught, Church-supported, goal-oriented gospel instruction. We are being asked to support Come, Follow Me and Children and Youth[5] in our homes. As mentors, we need to support the youths' role in leadership,[6] in the gathering of Israel, and in ministering.[7] It will take a measure of spiritual resilience for us to do so. The genius of the recent Church-wide adjustments pivots on the truth that everyone must listen to the Holy Ghost to make it work for individual families.

My hope is that as you learn of Nephi's spiritual journey and how it helped him develop spiritual resilience, you will feel more capable to overcome bad habits, resist temptations more effectively, recognize the Holy Ghost more often, and thereby more successfully teach the children in your care. We can do this! Christ helped Nephi, and He will help us.

CHAPTER SUMMARY

- *The book of Nephi contains the building blocks of spiritual resilience.*

- *We and our children need this spiritual resilience to prepare for the future.*

- *Our actions are our best teaching tool and honest indicators of our faith.*

- *The Holy Ghost will communicate with us as we ask ourselves introspective questions.*

"'Lord, what wilt thou have me to do?' A man can take
no greater action than to pursue a course that will bring
to him the answer to that question and then
to carry out that answer."

—Ezra Taft Benson[8]

Chapter 2

GOODLY PARENTS

What Is Parental Success?

"I, Nephi, having been born of goodly parents . . ."

—1 NEPHI 1:1

EVERY MEMBER OF NEPHI'S FAMILY reached the promised land[9] despite grave challenges and faithless missteps. That fact alone should bring us some hope, peace, and reassurance. Each of them certainly made mistakes, some very serious, yet still reached the promised land through repentance, forgiveness, and repeated efforts to be humble. It was a long process—a journey.

What did Lehi and Sariah do to support Nephi on his journey to becoming what the Lord needed him to be? From the beginning, Lehi and Sariah were commanded to teach Nephi and the rest of their family the gospel of Jesus Christ. The descriptions we are given of their teaching strategies are filled most frequently with their declarations of faith and their deep sacrifices to follow Christ. They taught their family with testimony and courage.[10]

Lehi clung to his faith in Christ and committed to do whatever Christ directed. He and his family did not survive the dangers of their day by avoiding challenges. Literally nothing except acknowledgment of God and His guidance led to their survival.[11] We cannot fully avoid stressful situations or complex decisions either. The goal of the Holy Ghost is not to maneuver us around roadblocks. His goal is to use these obstacles (and the eventual triumphs) to teach us truth in a way we will always remember.

Lehi's and Sariah's efforts to be obedient ensured that their children recognized they were choosing to follow Christ. They chose to sacrifice the security of a home and a comfortable life to follow Christ. And yet, in spite of all Lehi and Sariah did to set a good example, not all of their children partook of the fruit in Lehi's dream illustrating the tree of life.[12]

Many parents can relate to the frustration felt when a child cannot or will not recognize God's truth. While I have no doubt Laman and Lemuel possessed many good qualities, they were a continual source of worry and heartache to Lehi and Sariah. I am sure they contributed to the survival and happiness of their family. But the eternal consequences of their actions cannot be denied or rationalized away.

The continual complaint of Laman and Lemuel against Nephi was focused on the fact that he was "like unto [their] father, led away by the foolish imaginations of his heart" (1 Nephi 17:20). From 1 Nephi to the Book of Helaman, "foolish traditions" are invoked 42 times by the Lamanites as the anthem of continual warfare and bloodshed against the Nephites. The heartache of Lehi and Sariah was justified, but I do not believe it to be permanent.

Lehi had seen a vision of his posterity. He knew of the division within his family. He knew their disagreements would lead to bloodshed. He also knew about the coming of Christ and the redemptive power He would provide through forgiveness and knowledge. Lehi and Sariah knew their Savior had a plan in place for all their sons.

In some future day, the wisdom of developing lasting commitment through agency will be made perfectly clear to us. Nephi is taught this truth during one of the most poignant parts of the Book of Mormon. It starts with Nephi's vision of the full history and future of humanity, not necessarily in chronological order. First, maybe to support Nephi before he sees the bloodshed of his people, an angel shows Nephi the tree of life and the birth of the long-awaited Christ. Then Nephi sees the full consequences of his brothers' choices.

> And it came to pass that the angel said unto me: Look, and behold thy seed, and also the seed of thy brethren. And I looked and beheld the land of promise; and I beheld multitudes of people, yea, even as it were in number as many as the sand of the sea.
>
> And it came to pass that I beheld multitudes gathered together to battle, one against the other; and I beheld wars, and rumors of wars, and great slaughters with the sword among my people. (1 Nephi 12:1–2)

Mercifully, Nephi is next shown Christ's visit to the remnant of his people and the peace that their obedience would create. As the vision continues, Nephi is taught the destructive power of pride and the redemptive power of Christ. But he also witnesses the eventual hardening in the hearts of the Nephites, which would lead to their final destruction.

> And while the angel spake these words, I beheld and saw that the seed of my brethren did contend against my seed, according to the word of the angel; and *because of the pride of my seed*, and the temptations

of the devil, I beheld that the seed of my brethren did overpower the people of my seed. (1 Nephi 12:19, emphasis added)

Just as Nephi witnesses the wickedness of Laman and Lemuel leading to the harassment of the Nephites, he also witnesses the wickedness of the Nephites leading to their own destruction. While perhaps feeling heartbroken and devastated with this outcome, Nephi is then shown the second coming of Jesus Christ.

At the end of the vision, Nephi is returned to his present and immediately hears his brothers "disputing one with another" (1 Nephi 15:2). At this moment Nephi could have lashed out in frustration at his brothers' ignorance and the harm it would eventually cause, but he does not. How does his new knowledge inform his choice? Because Nephi knows his posterity is not lost to Christ, and because he knows people must choose for themselves, Nephi is able to act with charity toward his brothers. He experiences peace in Christ.

Nephi testifies to them with hope in the gathering of Israel and the great missionary work which will take place in the last days as those who doubted the gospel find their faith, repent, and return to the fold of Christ. Nephi is not just describing his seed or the seed of his brothers. He is describing *our* seed as well.

And now, the thing which our father meaneth concerning the grafting in of the natural branches through the fulness of the Gentiles, is, that in the latter days, when *our seed* shall have dwindled in unbelief . . .

And at that day shall the remnant of *our seed* know that they are of the house of Israel, and that they are the covenant people of the Lord; and then shall they know and come to the knowledge of their forefathers, and also to the knowledge of the gospel of their

Redeemer, which was ministered unto their fathers by him; where-fore, they shall come to the knowledge of their Redeemer and the very points of his doctrine, that they may know how to come unto him and be saved.

And then at that day will they not rejoice and give praise unto their everlasting God, their rock and their salvation? Yea, at that day, will they not receive the strength and nourishment from the true vine? Yea, will they not come unto the true fold of God?

Behold, I say unto you, Yea; they shall be remembered again among the house of Israel; they shall be grafted in, being a natural branch of the olive tree, into the true olive tree . . .

Wherefore, our father hath not spoken of our seed alone, but also of all the house of Israel. (1 Nephi 15:13–16; 18; emphasis added)

Our children will also be taught and gathered by their Savior.

Nephi knew the choices of his brothers would be consequential. He also knew he could not force his brothers to believe in the promises of Christ. Nephi knew he loved his brothers and wanted them to feel the joy and reassurance he felt through Christ. Therefore, his first take-away from experiencing that mighty vision was to teach his brothers that they were loved by God and would never be forgotten.

What does this teach us about how to treat our children? What example is set for us as we consider our effect on our posterity? Essentially, what is our measure of success? We cannot make decisions that our children must make for themselves. We *can* teach them "with all the feeling of a tender parent" (1 Nephi 8:37) the importance of the gospel. More importantly, we can make sure they know we love them. We can teach them that their Father in Heaven will always love them and wants to help them. We can commit to teaching the gospel in any way possible, knowing many hardships can be avoided through obedience.

When my girls were very young, we played a game they thought devilishly fun. We called the game "Would You Love Me?" They would ask, "Mom, would you love me if . . . ?" then come up with the silliest or naughtiest thing they could think of—everything from cutting a sister's hair to drawing on the couches to eating slugs.

I admit the game came with some risk. I still vividly remember learning the hazards of falling asleep during general conference. I woke up to find my three-year-old's permanent-marker handiwork all over the living room: couch, fireplace, walls . . . everything!

"Mommy, do you still love me?" she asked. Ahh!

The real benefit of the game came when they were older and their questions became a bit weightier. "Mom, would you still love me if I wrecked the car?" "Would you still love me if we didn't agree on anything?" "Would you still love me if I lied every day?" I was happy for every chance I got to tell them that my love did not depend on their actions.

The time it takes our children to learn the things they need to learn is longer than we can properly understand. Though difficult to remember and harder to imagine, their learning will last throughout this mortal life and their life hereafter. It's the same for us!

Eventually, through the patient teaching of our Savior and our own acts of repentance, all of us sinners will be grafted in, "being a *natural* branch of the olive tree" (1 Nephi 15:16). Our children, even if they struggle with their faith, will have an opportunity to find their rightful place with God—never to feel out of place again. They will be taught in a way that they can understand.

When Lehi spoke to Laman and Lemuel "with power, being filled with the Spirit, until their frames did shake before him" (1 Nephi 2:14), it was not to push them away. And when he "did cease speaking unto them" (1 Nephi 8:38), it was not because he had lost sight of their full potential. Even though they chose to disregard his teachings at that time, I believe Lehi was mindful that Laman and Lemuel were under the continual stewardship of Jesus Christ. Lehi had taught them the best he was able and trusted his Savior to teach his sons the rest.

The faith-filled decisions of our children are thrilling, but these decisions require consistent support. Their faithless decisions can hurt, but these are not the final words in their progression. We do not have the power to foresee the future outcome of their spirituality. We can only control whether we are doing what the Holy Ghost asks of us.

Remember, God's goal has never been limited to securing the obedience of His children. Just as all of Lehi's children did not partake of the tree of life, not all of our Heavenly Parents' children will partake of eternal life. God has the power to compel obedience from us or our children anytime He wishes, but He will never do so because it is antithetical to His very nature, as we know from both scriptures and revelation. A repeated show of His power could easily cower us into submission—and yet He doesn't work that way.

Instead, He allows agency—analysis and consequences, growth and remembrance. His focus has always been on teaching us what we need to know to progress and showing continual love along the way. Our loved ones are loved by One with more insight into what they need than we have ourselves. God understands His children's level of development and loves them in their strengths and weaknesses.[13] This is the measure of God's parental success! It can be the measure of our success as well.

Does the way we live the gospel, as well as the sacrifice we make, clearly display our highest priorities? Are we teaching the gospel with tenderness, being filled with the Spirit? What can that mean for us? Do our children know we love them regardless of whether or not they obey us?

Lehi and Sariah are good examples of the considerable patience and spiritual strength it takes to parent youth destined to be "God's heroes" (Nelson, 2018). Both Lehi and Sariah murmured at times because of the hard work asked of them. They were not free of mistakes or inadequacies. They accepted their placement in God's work and pressed forward. We shouldn't let this high bar discourage us. Instead, we can take comfort that we are not alone in our tasks, and we don't need to fear failure.

Through home-taught, Church-supported programs, Jesus Christ, along with His prophet, apostles, and servants, has placed more emphasis on the responsibility of parents to teach the gospel to this vital future generation. His faith in us is well-placed and well-guided. In fact, these adjustments can be interpreted as a boost of encouragement.

Time would not have been taken from our church meetings if Christ did not believe more personalized family instruction would be most instructive. We may feel ill prepared, that we have few options, or that we are strapped for time and resources. I contend that we have what we need for now—for the next few steps, at least.

We need to start where we are and teach what we can. Guidance will be provided for each step we take as we follow the counsel of our leaders. We can customize our teachings to fit our individual situations, interests and priorities. We can build our faith in the process and in ourselves as we go forth and do as we are asked. Let's not focus on what we aren't doing or can't do yet. Let's focus on what we can do and allow ourselves to grow more resilient.

The spiritual resiliency developed by teenage Nephi was also found in teenage Joseph Smith,[14] and it can be developed in the generations of tomorrow. There is a beautiful similarity between the childhood experiences of Nephi and Joseph we can apply to our youth today. Nephi and Joseph were taught the gospel primarily in their homes by faithful parents. President Nelson has asked us to focus on this sacred responsibility because Christ needs more "noble spirits" and the "finest players" (Nelson, 2018).

I too was born of "goodly parents." Just as Nephi, I have been taught from my birth "a great knowledge of the goodness and the mysteries of God" (Nephi 1:1). Mostly, I have tested, defended, and studied this knowledge throughout my life, but not always.

There have been times when I have avoided, disparaged, second-guessed, or disregarded these sacred truths. My life choices have not always been in my best interest. There were times I felt the gospel just didn't provide what I wanted. There were times when church didn't seem to have a place for me. There were times I thought I had a better answer. I have not always had a clear understanding of the risks I was taking or the divine guidance I was purposefully evading. Mostly, I just didn't want to think about it because the difficulty of the work seemed to outweigh the benefits.

In my late teens I recognized the "mists of darkness" (1 Nephi 12:17) getting thicker, obscuring my ability to make choices that led to beneficial outcomes. I did not find the "rod of iron" (1 Nephi 11:25) till I wanted to find it and went searching for it. I wanted to stop making ineffective choices. I wanted direction from God that I knew was better than the guesses in the dark I had been making. It wasn't until I studied the gospel myself and actively tested its promises that I gained the testimony I had seen displayed by my parents all along.

In 1 Nephi 8, we get the first description of the iron rod. It is a firm, immovable guide, available to all who find it, that leads the followers of Christ through the mists of darkness to the tree of life. What a beautiful concept! But what happens while a loved one is in the mists of darkness? How do we help our children find the iron rod or even *want* to find it?

In his dream, Lehi was "exceedingly fearful" as he walked across the "dark and dreary waste." He saw "a man . . . dressed in a white robe," whom he followed "for many hours" as he prayed for the "multitude of [the Lord's] tender mercies." Finally, Lehi beheld "a tree, whose fruit was desirable to make one happy" (1 Nephi 8:4–10).

After searching "that he might discover his family," Lehi beckoned them to the "rod of iron" and finally to the tree where he stood (1 Nephi 8:13–15). I love the example given in these verses. Lehi was led by Christ to where he needed to go and, even from afar, was able to lead his family to where they needed to go.

This scripture describes two sources of light, provided for us in our efforts to find the tree and lead our families to it.

Our first source of light is Christ. He is reliable and consistent. Christ has never and will never leave us in utter darkness. You are not without His light even now. The following question challenges us to prove otherwise:

Who is among you that feareth the Lord, that obeyeth the voice of his servant, that walketh in darkness and hath no light? (2 Nephi 7:10).

We are always given the information we need for even a small step in the right direction.

One year, I attended a Young Women high-adventure activity where I experienced a taste of utter darkness. We hiked more than a mile laterally through a lava tube and descended more than 250 feet vertically into pits with names like "The Devil's Throat." We hefted our climbing gear while scrambling over piles of boulders bigger than we were. That night we slept in absolute darkness within the cave.

Sharp-edged rocks, low ceilings, and deep trenches presented frequent hazards within the cave. I immediately recognized how pitch-black darkness can leave you with almost no choices. I either had a source of light or I did not. I could not step forward without it. There was no in between.

Never have I experienced such a complete lack of light. By the time we scrambled through the opening at "Satan's Teeth" and back into the light of day, I was ready to never sleep with the light off again! I now realize a good high adventure is one you are more afraid of after than before!

This state of total darkness need never apply to us spiritually because of the Atonement of Christ and the gift of the Holy Ghost. We need to understand that the Light of Christ is always illuminating our path forward. The next step necessary to bring us closer to our Father is always illuminated—for adults and children alike. The gospel of Christ is filling the world one person at a time, but His light is available to everyone. The question should not be whether the light is available, but whether we are recognizing these ideas as prompting from the Holy Ghost and following where they lead.

The Light of Christ can help us find the iron rod, but what about *wanting* to find it? As parents, as we emulate the Savior, we can become a second source of light for our youth. We have the opportunity to lead them to the iron rod and demonstrate why they should want to find and follow it. Our light can be effective even when we are not with them physically. Our testimonies and examples can create a source of light that illuminates the path for our children wherever they decide to go.

I have always been eager to participate in "night hikes." My youngest daughter inherited this same fascination. We've gone out late at night to experience a familiar world transformed into something adventurous in the dark, even in our pajamas! Usually, when walking at night, I tend to forgo the flashlight, knowing my night vision will get better the longer I am in the dark. Everyone around me usually has a flashlight anyway. My husband does not appreciate this idiosyncrasy of mine when I say things like, "I can see fine—it's bright enough for me," "If I let my eyes adjust to the dark, I can do it on my own," or, "I can see well enough I don't need your help!"

I can't recall how often I have conveyed some form of these same sentiments to my earthly parents and Heavenly Parents over the years: "I don't need to ask. I already know." "It doesn't feel bad at all." "I'm just as happy without it." "Why would I need that?" "If it's so important, why doesn't it resonate with me?" "It's not useful, anyway."

Have you ever walked down a dark trail as someone else shines a flashlight behind you? The beam of light helps you see, but only when your own body doesn't get in the way. The problem is not the light, which is constant, but your interaction with it. Often the light in this type of scenario creates annoyance and confusion as it cuts in and out.

While I was growing up, it seemed my parents were walking behind me wherever I went, holding up their testimonies like flashlights, helping me see where I was going. Their examples cast intermittent light on the choices I made. Sometimes I was annoyed with the comparisons between my choices and theirs. Tellingly, this only happened while I was walking in spiritual darkness and the light of their testimonies was intermittently obscured by my own perspective.

Our example can be a source of light for our children whether they are holding to the iron rod or wandering in the dark. Our children can be annoyed by the light cutting in and out and may even try to distort or block out our gospel teachings altogether. But every flash of light parents emit can remind children that Christ does not intend for us to walk in darkness. Indeed, we are born to be "children of the light" (2 Nephi 1:13; 1 Thessalonians 5:5–8).

Luckily, the consistency of a parent's testimony and example can provide just enough light for children to find their way forward and avoid some of the major obstacles in their paths until they develop their own testimonies—or carry their own flashlights, so to speak. Even though I have not lived in the same state as my parents for years, my daily actions reflect their examples. I *want* to be like them! I *want* to have the reassurance, peace, and purpose they have.

Because my parents relied heavily on His direction, I assume the Holy Ghost is actively trying to speak to me, rather than wonder if my thoughts are coming from just me. I dig deeper into the scriptures because I've seen my parents benefit from their teachings. I recognize those times I am being judgmental more quickly because my parents have willingly sacrificed for strangers knowing that each person they meet is a being of infinite worth. I reach out to the missionaries because of my dad's eagerness to share his testimony. I have not perfected my mother's skill for constantly seeking to fill the needs of those around her, but I still have time to work on it.

I cannot say that my parents' faith brought them an abundance of comfort. On the contrary, much like Lehi and Sariah, I'm sure their lives would have been more comfortable without their faith. Instead, my father's faith has made him fearless, even reckless at times. As a writer, advocate, and teacher, he is committed to bringing his fellow men to a knowledge of the gospel. Sleep, food, shelter, reputation, and even his safety have at times taken a backseat to his faith and desire to share what he knows with those around him.

My mother's faith has made her resilient. Not many would have had the fortitude she has exhibited in supporting her "visionary man." She's skillfully managed every aspect of caring for our large family and testified of the "goodness of God" at every opportunity. My mother has proven many times she believes following the promptings of the

Holy Ghost will always bring about the best results. Lehi exclaimed,

> I know that I am a visionary man; for if I had not seen the things
> of God in a vision I should not have known the goodness of God,
> but had tarried at Jerusalem, and had perished with my brethren. (1
> Nephi 5:4)

Lehi knew his visions saved his life and the lives of his family members. Laman and Lemuel believed Lehi's directions were lies, but not enough to stop them from walking through the desert or getting on the boat.

My father's steadfast faith and my mother's clear direction have saved my life in many ways. I sensed my parents knew that the Holy Ghost was leading me to "the goodness of God." I could have wandered onto dangerous paths in my teenage years without the lessons they taught me through their actions.

My parents never allowed me to wonder about their belief in the gospel of Jesus Christ. Their bright testimonies illuminated my choices, allowing me to see the danger I was in before I made a significant mistake. Despite the sullen, disrespectful attitude I had during my younger years, I could not help but recognize the flashes of clarity that brightened my life as I compared my actions to theirs.

The resiliency of my parents' testimonies is not something I regard as commonplace. Indeed, I see it as exceptional. Their light has been constant, and I have reaped the benefits of their efforts to live the gospel so valiantly. They have taught me about my Messiah, and He has taken away much of my fear. They showed me how their sense of security was not dependent on forces outside their control but rather on their faith in the Savior. Their example made me want to follow Him.

I now recognize the value of preaching the gospel as the priority, but also living in such a way as to demonstrate you believe it. The light of my testimony must shine brighter than did Laman's and Lemuel's if I wish to support the resilience of Nephi in my own children. As parents of a newer generation, we must turn up our own light.

We can take comfort in the fact that prophecy has declared that our children will not be destroyed like the Nephites or dwindle in unbelief like the Lamanites. Our posterity will usher in the coming of Christ and will succeed in uniting despite the strife of the latter days. They will need our best efforts to teach them our most important truths.

Chapter Summary

- *Christ gives us reason to hope even when our children choose a different path.*

- *We have a vital responsibility to teach the gospel in our homes.*

- *Our light is a more effective teacher than we realize.*

- *Our success comes by seeking the Holy Ghost and showing unconditional love.*

- *Action and commitment increase the brightness of our testimonies.*

"But the men and the women who are honest before God,
who humbly plod along, doing their duty, paying their tithing,
and exercising that pure religion and undefiled before God
and the Father, which is to visit the fatherless and the widows
in their afflictions and to keep oneself unspotted from the world,
and who help look after the poor; and who honor the holy
Priesthood, who do not run into excesses, who are prayerful
in their families, and who acknowledge the Lord in their hearts,
they will build up a foundation that the gates of hell cannot prevail
against; and if the floods come and the storms beat upon their house,
it shall not fall, for it will be built upon the rock of eternal truth."

—JOSEPH FIELDING SMITH[15]

Still shot of the brass plates by Book of Mormon Video Production. © By Intellectual Reserve, Inc. Courtesy of The Church of Jesus Christ of Latter-day Saints. Used by permission.

Chapter 3

ALL THE LEARNING OF MY FATHER

What Do You Already Know for Yourself?

"Therefore I was taught somewhat in all the learning of my father."

—1 NEPHI 1:1

IF WE'RE GOING TO DESIGNATE MORE TIME to teaching our children, what should we teach them? In many ways, we are still in the first verse of the first chapter of the first book in our efforts to figure out what "home-centered" means for our families. Nephi's journey began with the lessons his parents had learned for themselves. With the Come, Follow Me program, we have greater opportunities to teach our children the lessons we have learned for ourselves.

Our light shines brighter when we are sincere. Hypocrisy was the great evil of the Pharisees and Sadducees of Christ's day. No one will pick up on the hypocrisy of parents faster than their children.

It's okay to teach what we know while acknowledging what we do not. There are principles of the gospel we do not fully understand. We all have times when the honest answer to a question is "I don't know." We do not need to pretend, make excuses, become defensive, or otherwise act as if it is not true.

During Nephi's vision, the angel guiding him asks a question I have thought about many times, for I feel that there is a great deal of wisdom to be found in it: "Knowest thou the condescension of God?" In this instance, Nephi's answer is particularly applicable. "And I said unto him: I know that he loveth his children; nevertheless, I do not know the meaning of all things" (1 Nephi 11:16–17). Nephi is forthcoming about what he does know and what he does not. His inability to articulate the foundational meaning of Christ's sacrifice does not stop him from expressing his love of Christ, nor does it hinder his ability to gain a wealth of truth from Christ.

On the other hand, we offer our most persuasive testimony based on gospel principles we understand well. While the preparation that goes into a family lesson is beneficial, it does not trump relevance and personal insight. Who's to say that the lessons you have learned are not the precise messages your children need to hear? Our life lessons are taught most effectively when they are based on honest, personal experiences.

There is one major benefit of home-focused learning over Church-based teaching: feelings of doubt, tough or awkward questions, the acknowledgment of sins, and the principles of forgiveness can all be talked about in private, relatable ways in our homes as opposed to being spoken about in generalizations when in a group. We are able to discuss things that would be inappropriate among people outside our family.

Home-centered Come, Follow Me is the perfect setting to describe the specific application of faithful benefits. At our house we call it

"Awesome Hour." During this time you can relate your personal applications of the gospel of Christ. For example, you might share how you are making an added effort to ponder the scriptures as an act of appreciation for a specific blessing. You can lead a discussion on what you should focus on in a family prayer. You can ask for forgiveness and make amends, explaining how you might act differently next time. You can discuss the gospel question you are fasting about. You can testify about how a prompting helped you make progress in overcoming a harmful habit or avoiding a problem.

We could have done all of this before the shift to a more home-centered gospel study, of course, but now the opportunities can be more numerous. You can do it in a way that is more applicable to your family. With so many principles to teach and so many influences to counter, it can be difficult to know where to start and how to fit it all in. This is where you should rely on the Holy Ghost. It's His job to know the things you can't possibly know on your own.

I have found comfort in Lehi's example. Notice how, early in the story, Lehi recognizes he is overwhelmed and seeks support and direction from the Lord. Also notice the order of Lehi's actions. In 1 Nephi 1, knowing that everything is about to change, Lehi relies on the direction of the Lord. The people of Jerusalem are wicked, and his family is going to suffer because of factors outside his control.

> In that same year there came many prophets, prophesying unto the people that they must repent, or the great city Jerusalem must be destroyed." Lehi, "as he went forth, prayed unto the Lord, yea, even with all his heart, in behalf of his people. (1 Nephi 1:4–5)

Are not our children also surrounded by influences we cannot control? Lehi knew he needed help, but it did not stop him from going forth *as* he prayed. We need to be an example of what we want our youth to do. We should prayerfully take a step forward, pursue the direction received, and repeat. As we continue to go forth, we can again ask "in behalf of [our] people" what we need to do next. For me, answers are most often clarified *while* I'm taking those small steps forward, not before or after. I have come to know there are few topics God wants to discuss with us more than the welfare of our families.

Lehi receives a warning and immediately sets off into the wilderness to protect his family. We are not told whether he clearly saw the route in his mind or knew the destination. It is not evident that he knew they would travel to the coast or eventually sail a great distance over water. Regardless, he was so confident in whom he was following that in spite of his abundance he didn't even take money as a precaution against some future obstacle.

> And it came to pass that [Lehi] departed into the wilderness. And he left his house, and the land of his inheritance, and his gold, and his silver, and his precious things, and took nothing with him, save it were his family, and provisions, and tents, and departed into the wilderness. (1 Nephi 2:4)

He relied on Christ, his director and redeemer, and he put one foot in front of the other. His family members had to have faith in Lehi as their leader, as much as they needed to have faith in Christ as their director. I imagine there were plenty of days that, in walking through the hot desert, Lehi and Sariah asked, "Are we on the right track? Are we going the right way?"

I imagine they often got the same answer I sometimes receive: "You're doing well; just keep going." When faced with hardships (in their case, exposure, starvation, and dehydration), that answer can feel insufficient. Let us trust God to tell us when to make a turn, and let us listen when He does tell us. Our children and our spouses need to know they can trust us to listen to the Spirit as we lead our families. That trust is developed through honesty, consistency, and humility before God.

I never knew my paternal grandfather. George M. Papa, Sr. died before I was born, but his humility before God is legendary. Grandpa Papa grew up in a family of Croatian bootleggers, supplying the Chicago mobs of the 1930s, but after marrying my grandmother, he was baptized a member of The Church of Jesus Christ of Latter-day Saints. The two later moved to Snowflake, a small town in Northern Arizona. I can't imagine that his new father-in-law was very impressed to see Mr. Papa holding the hand of his only beloved daughter.

To say George was rough around the edges would be merely scratching the surface. He had smoothed some of his rough corners but was still a mighty proud man—except when it came to God. To his God he was submissive, and he listened when God spoke.

When George Papa, Sr., was finally ready to commit to God, he wasn't going to let much stand in his way. He and my grandmother, with her parents and their first baby boy, were so excited to take the long bus ride from Snowflake, Arizona to Salt Lake City, Utah to be endowed and sealed as a family. They waited by that bus stop, luggage in hand. They waited and waited and waited a little more. Finally, they decided the bus wasn't going to come that day after all. While the rest of the family decided to walk back to the house, George hesitated.

"I'm going to wait here," he said, "just to see what happens." Not even fifteen minutes went by before an older woman drove up and stopped in front of him.

"Sir, you know the bus isn't coming today, right?" I imagine her saying.

"Yes, ma'am."

"Sir, would you like to buy my car?"

Within ten minutes, the car ownership was exchanged for the exact amount George had in his pocket. He swung by the house to pick up his family. The car already had a full tank of gas. They headed to the temple to make covenants they knew they could keep.

Years later, George received a phone call saying his father was dying and he should come quickly if he wished to see him again. George, my grandmother, and their three young sons piled into their rundown car and headed for Chicago. Somewhere in the deserts of New Mexico, the car gave out. I have plenty of experience in hot deserts, so I can vividly imagine the swirling grit, baking heat, and blinding light whenever I think of this story.

My grandfather stepped away from the car and prayed to his God. Obeying the direction he received, he started walking into the desert and traveled over the hills, where he found an abandoned car sticking up out of the sand. Once he'd removed the carburetor and miraculously installed it in his own disabled car, away they went. Many examples such as this taught the sons of George Sr.—including my father—the benefits of making spiritually resilient choices.

What has your family come to expect from you when a decision needs to be made? What would they see as your typical reaction to change, hardship, generosity, or repentance? Can they reasonably expect you to lead them to their land of promise?

If that last question feels heavy, take heart. We are mistake-makers, which is precisely how God planned for it to be! It is no surprise to Him that we are beginning our journey toward perfection and nowhere near the end. My grandfather has been described as residing well past the imperfect category and closer to the lost-soul category, but he did not try to hide that fact from his God. He humbly asked for and received guidance, improved his character, and taught his sons by his example. This is how the divinely appointed system of families should work. God needs us to demonstrate to our children the genuine humility of repentance as much as the strength of spiritual resilience.

We all falter, and often our weaknesses involve selfishness, unkindness, or pride. This does not negate our efforts toward repentance, humility, charity, and learning. Our own doubts, questions, or shortcomings can be real, but our efforts, testimonies, and promptings are just as real. One does not cancel out the other. Both sides can coexist while we actively implement the Atonement in our lives and seek personal revelation for continual spiritual growth.

Let's go back to Lehi and his family. After traveling some distance, Lehi still did not know where he was going. However, he did not focus on what he did not know. He focused on what he *did* know: the Lord had a plan for his family. For this, Lehi was grateful.

> And it came to pass that when he had traveled three days in the wilderness, he pitched his tent in a valley by the side of a river of water. And it came to pass that he built an altar of stones, and made an offering unto the Lord, and gave thanks unto the Lord our God. (1 Nephi 2:6–7)

We may wish for a better understanding of Church history, plural marriage, same-sex attraction, our Heavenly Mother, our roles in heaven, and other topics which have further explanation. This desire for more information can reside alongside our gratitude for the knowledge we *do* have of resurrection, immortality, forgiveness, covenant blessings, divine families, and the plan of salvation. We can trust God's process, knowing more insight will be shared when we better understand what we have already been given.

Do our children assume we have everything figured out? Why would they? As parents, we need to feel more comfortable in discussing with our children the strengths and weaknesses in our testimonies in a humble and honest way, always acknowledging our progress toward Christ and greater understanding. Our children will certainly have similar ups and downs. In order to make progress, they need to be prepared for a journey that requires persistence. If they see only our strengths, they will not understand what to do when they feel weak.

Youth often wonder things like whether they can ever be useful to God or marry in the temple after making a big mistake. They don't want to admit it when they don't understand fasting or garments or chastity. They often feel a sin can cancel our love for them, or even God's love for them. They fear acknowledging that they have questions, not wanting to disappoint us.

We need to be more specific about how the Atonement has made a reliable difference when we've fallen short. It may help our children feel more comfortable talking to us about their struggles if we show humility and honesty about our own.

When I was about thirteen years old, I was snooping through my mother's things and found a journal she had written as a teenager. As I was skimming through the pages, I read a surprising passage about her and a boy she liked. In her teenage voice, she wrote about how she immediately knew she was in a bad situation and walked away from temptation, knowing she did not want to be near it again.

When I got older, I found the courage to talk to her about a compromising situation of my own. Learning from her honest retelling was what helped me speak up. I didn't feel as ashamed in talking to her about it because I felt she understood what I was going to say. It brought me comfort to know that my mother, who is an excellent example of virtue, had some of the same teenage concerns I did. I thought, "Maybe there's hope for me after all."

Chapter Summary

- *We should be honest and sincere in what we teach.*

- *Our families will better trust our leadership as we consistently rely on the Spirit.*

- *We must be open and humble about our use of and need for the Atonement.*

- *We should expect imperfection while we progress.*

"Please don't nag yourself with thoughts of failure.
Do not set goals far beyond your capacity to achieve.
Simply do what you can do, in the best way you know,
and the Lord will accept of your effort."

—GORDON B. HINCKLEY[16]

Chapter 4

WHEREFORE CAN YE DOUBT?

What Is Spiritual Resilience?

"Wherefore can ye doubt? Let us go up; the Lord is able to deliver us, even as our fathers."

—1 NEPHI 4:3

MANY EXAMPLES OF RESILIENCE are showcased in nature: the sturdy oak adapting to the mighty winds by digging deeper roots; the oceanside cliff standing resolute against the crashing waves; a tiny spark never failing to light up the surrounding dark. Resilience describes one's ability to stay true to form, retain purpose, and remain committed despite challenges, circumstances, and pressures.

Even though they lived in the same family and heard the same truths, there were some distinct differences between Nephi and his brothers. The sons of Nephi had different levels of spiritual resilience. Why were these differences so impactful? What did Nephi and Sam know that Laman and Lemuel did not? Nephi and Sam saw God's direction as an opportunity for progress worthy of the cost, while Laman and Lemuel prized their reasoning over that of God. Nephi and Sam were willing, confident in their abilities, and eager for the next steps. Laman and Lemuel wanted to be convinced before making an effort. They wanted God to work for them, rather than wanting to work for God.

Lehi endured the constant murmuring of Laman and Lemuel during their arduous journey between Jerusalem and the Red Sea. At one point, Lehi told Laman, "O that thou mightest be like unto this river, continually running into the fountain of all righteousness!" (1 Nephi 2:9). And to Lemuel, "O that thou mightest be like unto this valley, firm and steadfast, and immovable in keeping the command- ments of the Lord!" (1 Nephi 2:10). In other words, Lehi was pleading for more spiritual resilience in his oldest sons. He was begging them to be of a stronger, more consistent faith.

What is spiritual resilience? It's a measure of strength, single-mind- edness, hope, determination, and endurance that consistently answers the Savior's call for action.

Spiritual resilience is what allowed Daniel to walk into the lion's den[17] and prompted the boy Samuel to answer, "Speak; for thy servant heareth" (1 Samuel 3:10). It is the virtue that inspired Mary to testify with such grace and self-assurance.[18] It is the wise resolve that kept Mormon morally clean despite his surroundings.[19] It is the fearless trait that allowed David to stand his ground while holding nothing more than a rock and sling in his hands.[20] Esther gathered her spiritual resilience through the support of her people before risking her own life to save theirs.[21] Isaac climbed onto the sacrificial altar with more than blind obedience.[22]

Each of these heroes had a spiritual resilience that anchored them in their trust of God. They were young, yet they were led by the Holy

Ghost. They were inexperienced and imperfect, yet they were not overwhelmed by their role in God's work. They all chose to take a confident step forward. Live or die, these young people must have made a decision similar to one spoken about some millennia earlier by the mighty prophet Enoch:

Choose you this day, to serve the Lord God who made you. (Moses 6:33)

Is it possible Nephi gained strength from this same scripture? Nephi describes the murmuring of Laman and Lemuel as a direct result of them not knowing "the dealings of that God who had created them" (1 Nephi 2:12). In his final plea to his sons, Lehi emphasized the humbling knowledge that "there is a God, and he hath created all things, both the heavens and the earth, and all things that in them are" (2 Nephi 2:11). An understanding of who Christ is, what He is capable of, what we owe Him, and what He wants for us can give us the resolve to follow Him and the endurance we need to weather the trials that come our way.

Again, the first verse of the first book in the Book of Mormon describes the foundation Nephi's faith education:

Having seen many afflictions in the course of my days, nevertheless, having been highly favored of the Lord in all my days; yea, having had a great knowledge of the goodness and the mysteries of God. (1 Nephi 1:1)

How can this not be the best place for us to start? A thorough understanding of God's plan for us and of His involvement in our lives is a determining factor when it comes to the endurance of our faith. Christ declared His spiritual resilience on the cross as "not my will, but Thine, be done" (Luke 22:42). The years of growth Christ experienced before making the ultimate sacrifice were guided by a firm knowledge that He was "about His Father's business" (Luke 2:49). The knowledge of His importance in God's plan strengthened His resolve to perform His sacred duties.

Jesus's cousin, John the Baptist, was dedicated to his mission at a young age, living apart in the desert and teaching of Christ the Messiah and preparatory repentance.[23] His resilience was due in part to a prophecy of his father, Zacharias, at his birth, wherein he referenced the fulfillment of the covenant of Abraham, saying, "And thou, child, shalt be called the prophet of the Highest: for thou shalt go before the face of the Lord to prepare His ways" (Luke 1:76).

From the time they were children, these men knew they had a sacred role to play, and this knowledge played a part in their developing a resilience resplendent before their God, which carried them through unimaginable trials. Their efforts and eternal success deserve our utmost praise.

Understanding the plan of salvation and our placement in it can be a determining factor in the durability of our faith. In my work with the youth and with family and friends, I have witnessed a recurring theme: Not recognizing one's personal place in God's plan of salvation can be the first stumbling block to developing spiritual resilience. The youth need to have a broader understanding of what it means to be a son or daughter of God and member of The Church of Jesus Christ of Latter-day Saints. They need to be sure there is a role prepared for each one of them.

I remember a conversation I had years ago with a once-faithful family member. I was caught up in defending my faith, saying that I knew God could perform a miracle if He so chose. God had created the worlds. Could He not also perform a miracle of healing? In an unintentionally condescending way, this family member explained what he saw as faults in my reasoning. He asked whether I had any understanding of the massive power required to create a world, meaning it was unreasonable to believe one being could hold such power.

"Is that not the type of power you could at least respect?" I countered.

"God needs to show up sometimes," he responded.

In that moment, the Holy Ghost brought to my mind all the respect and love I had for this person, and I was able to say, "I see God in you."

For this family member, there was no acceptance of the works of God as testified within the scriptures, no recognition of God's daily influence in our lives. If there had been, my conversation with him would have gone differently. Instead, it seemed he felt that God had left the equation or perhaps God had provided an equation without giving us enough information to solve it. If God had so much power, where were the results?

I wanted him to know God had "showed up" in him, through him, and because of him. I saw all the brilliance, generosity, capability, and good intention this man had exemplified throughout my life. I saw a glimpse of his placement in God's work and knew he was doing his best to fulfill all the good he could offer his fellow man.

This conversation took less than a few minutes, but I have remembered it many times because of the interjection of the Holy Ghost. I gained a powerful witness of how God feels about each of us, whether we see eye to eye with Him, reciprocate his love, or even know Him yet. He loves us beyond mortal comprehension, but when we can catch even a glimpse of His love for us, we know this love is powerful enough to bring great results in our lives and in the lives of those we are striving to teach and guide.

As parents, we need to work on making sure that our children can visualize their individual placement in God's plan. They should be able to recognize a part of God in themselves. They should see not just a vague, general outline, but a personal, customized fit framed within the plan of salvation. Yes, we have divine *potential*, but our divinity is not simply reserved for a future date. We have it and can cherish it now. We can see the best parts of ourselves through the context of God's purposes.

Who knows a child's strengths and weaknesses better than their parents? Who can better recognize how that child's most frustrating traits can become their greatest assets if shifted toward righteous application? Who is better qualified to help our children see their place in God's plan than we are? We are best qualified to help our children know that God has an outcome for them that is uniquely fulfilling.

With a reliance on the Holy Ghost and a recognition of God's attention, love, and respect for our youth, we can help them see how they fit into God's plan. Our children may not always recognize their strengths, or they may be afraid their strengths do not fit into a preconceived mold. They may not be able to see how a personal strength can positively impact their future.

Christ wants to add His insight into how we fit within the plan of salvation. Our opportunity for a patriarchal blessing is one way He does this. There is a reason why this most personal communication from our Savior focuses on our placement and interaction within His plan of salvation. Encourage your youth to not delay receiving this boost of confidence and clarity so critically needed in their teenage years.

Perhaps the way we talk of righteousness is part of why youth often feel they don't fit in. They have expressed it as unobtainable or oppressive rather than supportive and liberating. Yes, the path of righteousness has been described as strait and narrow, but Christ has the power to include all people within His plan. Therefore, our path must be led by the Holy Ghost with consideration of each of us individually.

Throughout the scriptures, the Lord uses various images to help us understand the meaning and importance of being righteous. Some of the most referenced include a "rod of iron" (1 Nephi 8:24), a singular "doorway" (Revelation 3:8), and a "strait and narrow path" leading to a "gateway" that allows all who enter to find peace (3 Nephi 27:33).

Maybe you're like me. I used to think these images felt exclusive, out of reach, or inhibiting, as if I couldn't be good enough to get to them. As if even once I was there, I wouldn't be able to be myself. But I was thinking of them in the wrong way. In reality, these images are lovingly designed to help each one of us understand the Lord's message and how it is actually inclusive of all.

The iron rod represents the scriptures and teaches us that all who cling to them can safely reach their destination, no matter where they are along the rod. The doorway represents Christ, whose infinite sacrifice for all gives us access to God and immortality while retaining our true form in the process. The gateway represents our covenants, which endow all obedient Saints equally with plenty of capacity.

These images are not only critical if we hope to understand the need for careful reliance on Christ, they also demonstrate Christ's love for all of us. We must understand that Christ is the only source of all that is good and righteous.[24] He is the only way anyone can return to our Heavenly Parents.

These images represent our goals, but how do we reach those goals from where we are right now?

First, we must find the iron rod. We must get on the path. We must reach the door. How do we get there? Where does getting on that strait and narrow path start for you? Does it start in the same place for me? Or for your child?

Instead of seeing the covenant path as a single, crowded road leading up a mountainside, we can imagine many paths starting from several places around the base of the same mountain. All of them are straight and narrow, and all lead upward, but each starts from a different location. All of them cross different terrain, and all need navigation. All are guided by the Holy Ghost; all are supported by Christ's grace and the covenants we make with Him. All lead to God's kingdom on the mountaintop.

> And it shall come to pass in the last days, when the mountain of the Lord's house shall be established in the top of the mountains, and shall be exalted above the hills, and *all nations shall flow unto it.*
>
> And many people shall go and say, *Come ye, and let us go up to the mountain of the Lord,* to the house of the God of Jacob; and *he will teach us of his ways,* and *we will walk in his paths*; for out of Zion shall go forth the law, and the word of the Lord from Jerusalem. (2 Nephi 12:2–3; emphasis added)

In this scriptural description, I appreciate how "all nations" represents various starting points. Notice how *ways* and *paths* are plural rather than singular. That is an important message: We should not expect our children to learn the gospel the same way we do.

Christ has enough love, compassion, and understanding to provide a path that is perfect for each person. And parents can teach their children that even if they encounter a spiritual roadblock in their way, it is possible to adjust, maneuver and continue their climb. Through fasting and prayer, everyone can know what their next step should be.

Our modern prophets have taught us continually to be compassionate and seek to understand others. The new Children and Youth program encourages youth to focus on personal goals and interests. Christ wants us to recognize that we do not need to fit the same mold to be part of His plan. We are not collective Mormons, but Latter-day Saints.

In fact, our individual skills will be the key to expanding His kingdom on the earth. As we follow the training of the prophet and the map provided by the Holy Ghost, we can better visualize how our individual traits fit into Christ's plan of salvation. He wants our specialized capabilities and accepts our personal routes to testimony and our faithful expressions. He wants us to learn to be guided in more detailed, personal ways. He then wants us to share our gained insights with others, helping them feel at home with the gospel of Christ, regardless of their background, location, or life experiences.

We need to take time to make sure our children understand that the plan of salvation—the foundation of spiritual resilience—applies to all while providing individual application. Almost every question can be clarified when seen through the lens of the plan of salvation.

Let's take the young woman who dreams of making an impact on the world, or the one who loves science and could happily study the rest of her days. She may be creative, capable, self-driven, and intelligent. These traits will serve her well for the rest of her life. Should she question her belonging in church specifically, or the plan of salvation generally, if she wants to pursue a career or doctorate instead of raising a family right now? Certainly not. Why?

First, as she lives her covenants, she can be assured the Holy Ghost is leading her. Her promptings may lead her in an unexpected direction, but never the wrong one.[25] Second, her righteous interests are given by her Heavenly Parents to lead her back to Them. As parents, we can ensure she understands that her Heavenly Parents love her and have a special, individualized role for her to play that coordinates with her unique traits. As we help her recognize and rely on specific direction from the Holy Ghost, she will be able to make these important decisions the right way.

Following the Holy Ghost is the only way to find the path that is the most fulfilling for this young woman. She may be led to follow her career and feel confident in doing so, or she may be helped to understand why her family should be her focus, or she may be guided as to how she can do both. Maybe a fourth option will be made clear, one that is specifically prepared for her. Following the personal inspiration she receives from the Holy Ghost will leave her feeling confident about the path she chooses.[26]

Wouldn't it be nice to know which option is best? Unsurprisingly, our Heavenly Father wants us to know. That's why he has provided the Holy Ghost to lead us on our individual path directly to Christ.

I have met youth and parents who are struggling to understand the Church's policies and teachings pertaining to chastity, church discipline, same-sex attraction, and gender equality. How does the plan of salvation apply in these scenarios? At one point in my prayers for greater understanding on these issues, I was prompted by the Holy Ghost to study two chapters of scripture that helped me better understand the value every individual brings to accomplishing God's purposes. I have been reassured to find that others who have studied these related questions have also been led to these chapters.

The first chapter I studied was Moroni 8. The doctrine found therein states that all children are born sinless, that all have the fullest potential, and that all are "alive in Christ." All children are born with the capacity to receive exaltation.

The second chapter I studied was 1 Corinthians 12. In it we learn how to become united with Christ, or "of one body." To do so, we must "honour" each "member" of the whole until there is "no schism in the body." Even those whose faith seems "to be more feeble, are necessary." Only after recognizing, valuing, and respecting each different yet critical contribution of others can the combined experience of all teach us of Christ's comprehensive charity and purpose.

The youth who are eager to find innovative strategies have a great deal they could teach me about following the inspiration of the Holy Ghost. A person who experiences same-sex attraction and strives to obey the law of chastity has a great deal to teach me about whether Christ comforts those in need of comfort. A mother with a large family has a great deal to teach me about anchoring our hope in Christ. A black man who was denied ordination in the 1960s has a great deal he could teach me about waiting patiently on the Lord. A convicted criminal who struggles through repentance has a great deal she could teach me about the redemption of Christ. A terminally-ill family member has a great deal she could teach me about the value of life. A consistent ministering brother has a great deal to teach me about the rewards of dedicated service. A family that has lost their home has a great deal they could teach me about seeking help in our daily struggles. All these voices and personal experiences can educate us about a different aspect of Christ's power and interaction.

We are still learning the eternal significance of being male and female. We are still learning the cost of sin and why Christ has dictated specific standards. We *do* know Christ has promised fulfilling purpose, joyful forgiveness, and eternal agency to all those who follow and trust Him. As we more fully share and learn of diverse experiences in these latter days, we will come to better understand the plan of salvation. I encourage you to read and pray about Moroni 8 and 1 Corinthians 12. Determine what truths may apply to your situation or how to better answer the questions youth will ask.

Teenagers today will pursue spiritual resilience more wholeheartedly when they know God's plan is prepared for them specifically and inclusively. They will not fully recognize the power of Christ's love unless they can see that His love extends to the people around them. The youth of today must learn to use the plan of salvation more often. Remember Enoch and his holy city. It was once a large population riddled with sin and in need of redemption.[27] Every single one of them, including their youth, must have come to know that the plan of salvation would work for them before they were faithful enough to repent and finally translated. I believe their working unitedly was the key to their success.

I gain such hope from the optimism of our prophets and apostles. They are not weighed down by fear of division, wickedness, and strife. Their hearts are not failing them. No, our prophets are hopeful and maybe even eager for the last days. Why? I believe it is because they know that the youth of today have the tools necessary to develop more spiritual strength and obtain more answers with each passing challenge.

In August 2019, Douglas D. Holmes of the Young Men General Presidency said of today's youth, "We've been all around the world, and, I think for all of us, we always walk away amazed at the strength, the testimony and the depth of insight and understanding that the youth have in their commitment to the gospel. But we also see the reality of their struggles in modern culture, and while they're different around the world, the world has become a lot smaller place in our electronic age. They are, in some ways, also facing very similar challenges."[28]

I interpret this to mean that in the coming days, an ever-growing number of faithful Saints will be working together to solve an ever-diminishing number of spiritual riddles. Our place in the history of humanity is to be part of a world that's filled with an abundance of pure knowledge. Significant and varied tools can be leveraged for great testimonial power.

Chapter Summary

- *Spiritual resilience is the strength required to do the Lord's will.*

- *Not understanding God's plan of salvation undermines the development of resilience.*

- *Our children need us to help them visualize their personalized place in His plan.*

- *Consider how the plan of salvation addresses each of our doctrinal questions.*

"I testify to you that our promised blessings are beyond measure.
Though the storm clouds may gather,
though the rains may pour down upon us,
our knowledge of the gospel and
our love of our Heavenly Father and of our Savior
will comfort and sustain us and bring joy to our hearts
as we walk uprightly and keep the commandments. . . .
The future is as bright as your faith."

—THOMAS S. MONSON[29]

Chapter 5

Soften My Heart

How Can You Develop Spiritual Resilience?

"I did cry unto the Lord; and behold he did visit me, and did soften my heart that I did believe all the words which had been spoken by my father."

—1 Nephi 2:16

Over many years, many of my hours have been spent caring about the young people around me, especially those who've faced hardships I never imagined. These youth have faced serious health issues, mental illness, betrayal, financial hardship, and lack of support—sometimes dealing with such adversities all at once.

One of these youth closed the door on those reaching out to them, while another quietly acknowledged each person's efforts. One of them pulled away from church, while another sought after testimonial support like a thirsty man seeks water. One of them didn't want to hear about how gospel understanding could help make sense of their situation, while another openly described the gospel applications within new obstacles and thanked God for each sliver of silver lining. The weight these teenagers were carrying, often alone, was intense. How proud I was of each of them for carrying this weight to the best of their abilities. How I wanted to lift their burdens for them.

Spiritual resilience was the determining factor when it came to their testimonies. Some of these youth had parents who faithfully supported them, while others did not. If parents were setting the example of acting on their faith it was much more likely for struggling teens to retain or regain their testimonies. If parents were betraying the trust placed in them it seemed the testimony of the child was rolling down a hill, too fast to be caught.

All the youth I have worked closely with—even those who did not find the answers they wanted—have had a heightened capacity intrinsic to their characters. You may have heard this often, and you will hear it again: there is something unique about the youth of today. I echo our prophet's belief that the youth of today have a greater capacity for wisdom, deeper conversion, and more inspired leadership than the youth of any other generation.

Their hearts are simply more open. They want to be influential and to make a difference. They are often focused on blessing those around them. You may say, "I wish that described my kid." Don't be surprised if your child surprises you!

A few months ago, my teenage daughter, Natalie Goettl, gave a talk in sacrament meeting about a spiritual insight she gained from the first few chapters in Nephi. This was one of those instances where her perspective helped educate the adults in the chapel that day. (I should add that it left her mom feeling quite impressed!)

I will quote her words here in respect for her spiritual preparation but also to highlight the capacity of this rising generation for insight and wisdom:

Lehi and his family are in the wilderness, and Laman and Lemuel were complaining against their father and the Lord, then Lehi commands them to have faith. Nephi is watching this, and he's confused about who is right—his father or his brothers. So he goes and prays about it.

We always view Laman and Lemuel as the bad guys of the Book of Mormon. They were complaining and arguing, and they lost trust in the Lord because they were more focused on earthly things. Then we look over at Nephi and we see this hero, this perfect being who never lost trust and never did anything wrong and was always righteous.

But the thing is, Nephi, Laman, and Lemuel are all very similar. They share almost the same experiences. The key difference between them, which is why I feel we view them to be the villains and heroes of the Book of Mormon, is even though they went through the same experiences, the way they responded to those experiences and the choices they made, made all the difference.

In 1 Nephi 2:16, it says, "And it came to pass that I, Nephi, being exceedingly young, nevertheless being large in stature, and also having great desires to know of the mysteries of God, wherefore, I did cry unto the Lord; and behold he did visit me, and did soften my heart that I did believe all the words which had been spoken by my father; wherefore, I did not rebel against him like unto my brothers."

A couple of important lines stuck out to me as I was reading this, such as, "having great desires to know the mysteries of God." I love that line. [*Note*: this is one of Natalie's whys, which I explain later.] When you sincerely pray, you need to have a desire and a will to learn and accept how God is going to respond. That curiosity and willing-ness Nephi was feeling were key. God's not going to answer if you are just mildly curious about something. You must pray with real intent. And that is exactly what Nephi did. He made the choice to ask.

That is what is so different about Nephi and Laman and Lemuel. Nephi reached out to the Lord faithfully, and he was blessed with the truth. We can be blessed with knowing the truth, too, if we only reach out and ask.

The next line is, "and behold he did visit me, and did soften my heart." That revelation was given to Nephi as a result of his trust. Nephi's heart was softened by the answers given to him through God. Something I was shown in seminary a couple days ago really stuck out to me. Nephi says that his heart was softened.

The thing is, you can't soften a heart that's already soft. Meaning that when Nephi heard what his father was saying, he was probably just as troubled as Laman and Lemuel were. He didn't immediately respond with, "Oh yeah, this is totally fine. I completely understand why I must do this. Traveling through the wilderness for years is gonna be so much fun. Let's go, guys!" No, he was probably confused and scared. He was just a kid. I'm guessing he was having some of the same thoughts as his older brothers. His home was being taken away from him, and he was leaving behind his life and everything he knew. His faith was probably wavering a bit.

In our lives, when our faith is wavering and trials come up, we have a choice. We can either choose to be like Laman and Lemuel and keep our struggles to ourselves, refusing to reach out to God. Or we can be like Nephi. When we're having doubts, we can choose to ask for help. Having doubts in our own mind doesn't mean that God is wrong. We can all go forward with the assumption that God loves us and will guide us.[30]

Natalie is in the process of developing spiritual resilience. Her talk describes the beginnings of Nephi's growing spiritual resilience, as understood by one of God's future heroes. This is the first time God shows Nephi facing a challenge. Nephi's resilience is developing; he is asking God in faith. Was this not the first step in Joseph Smith's building of resilience as well?

As Nephi grew older, he articulated this truth to his brothers:

Do ye not remember the things which the Lord hath said?—If ye will not harden your hearts, and ask me in faith, believing that ye shall receive, with diligence in keeping my commandments, surely these things shall be made known unto you. (1 Nephi 15:11)

There is spiritual wisdom here for us as we guide our children toward living with greater recognition of spiritual realities. There is great power in asking questions of the Lord. It shows we have faith that He will provide the answers. As exemplified by Nephi, we must pray with a true desire to know the mysteries of God if He is to soften our hearts so we can be led.

We can ask God, "What lesson does my child need to first learn in order to make progress?" As we ask in humility and with real intent (even if we're just seeking to know the mysteries of a teenage mind), God, in His great knowledge and understanding of our child, can give us the insight we seek for our child and our situation.

And we can share what we learn with that child. It is powerful when we can honestly and sincerely say, "I prayed for God to help me better understand what I can do to help you right now. This is what He told me to do." This is what I did in praying for my own children. This book is my version of the answer He gave me. It's my attempt at putting the doctrine of Christ into action.

While Children and Youth encourages the youth to say their own prayers, it also encourages them to ask the same questions: Lord, what do I need to do right now? What would you have me do first? If these questions are being asked in their prayers, they will be guided on what to do when their hearts need softening.

First Nephi 3:7 captures Nephi at the moment he is faced with another daunting "upward climb." But this time, Nephi has a history of interaction with God to rely on. He grasped a portion of "the mysteries of God who created [him]." He applied the doctrine of Christ to himself. Instead of needing his heart softened, Nephi voices words full of spiritual resilience.

Nephi's testimony provides a blueprint for how his *teenage* testimony works for him. He expresses purpose, hope, truth, and faith—but most importantly, his testimony moves him to action:

> And it came to pass that I, Nephi, said unto my father: I will go and do the things which the Lord hath commanded, for I know that the Lord giveth no commandments unto the children of men, save he shall prepare a way for them that they may accomplish the thing which he commandeth them. (1 Nephi 3:7; emphasis added)

This is my favorite scripture, and it marks the mileposts of Nephi's spiritual growth. What happened between 1 Nephi 2:16 and 1 Nephi 3:7? Nephi went from "great desire," "did believe," and the minimal "did not rebel," to the much stronger testimony of "I will go and do . . . for I know."

What questions did Nephi ask, and what answers did he receive that enabled him to respond in such a spiritually resilient way? How can his words support us in being who Christ needs us to be? Nephi's spiritual resilience became strong enough to save his family, embark across an ocean, and establish a nation. What can spiritual resilience do for us?

In the next five chapters, we will focus on this one verse by reverse-engineering Nephi's testimony to determine the questions he may have asked and the answers that supported his testimony. If finding the answers to these questions helped Nephi build spiritual resilience, then finding the answers to these same questions can help us and our youth build spiritual resilience as well.

I'll highlight five key phrases within this verse to help you understand the building blocks of Nephi's strength.

I will—Nephi was willing to promise. What have you promised to do?

Go and do—Nephi acted on what the Lord asked of him. What is asked of you?

For I know—Nephi knew why he was following Christ. Why do you follow Him?

He shall prepare—Nephi trusted the Lord. What has Christ prepared for you?

That they may accomplish—Nephi accomplished eternal outcomes. Can you recognize the significance of the spiritual direction you are given?

Nephi's verse requires us to ask deeply personal questions of ourselves—questions that will help us know where we need to focus to build spiritual resilience and, in turn, help our children to do the same.

My progress is made most quickly through heavenly answers to my mortal questions. If you do not have an answer to any of these questions, it's okay to say, "I don't know," or even, "I have never known." Doing so indicates where to start your focus. My hope is to be helpful as you find your own path forward from exactly where you are right now in your own situation.

Perhaps you already have answers to these questions based on your spiritual experience. Share these insights with your children, then let them come up with their own answers to these questions.

CHAPTER SUMMARY

- *Youth have a great capacity for spiritual insight.*

- *Humbly asking questions can produce softened hearts.*

- *Nephi's testimony in 1 Nephi 3:7 is a framework for his spiritual resilience.*

- *We can build spiritual resilience by focusing on areas we need to improve.*

"When obedience ceases to be an irritant and becomes our quest,
in that moment God will endow us with power."

—Ezra Taft Benson[31]

Chapter 6

I Will

What Have You Promised to Do?

"And it came to pass that I, Nephi, said unto my father: I will."

—1 Nephi 3:7

I will is a phrase full of conviction. When we say it, there should be no doubt we are committed to an outcome. The final accomplishment is real to us. Therefore, to say "I will" requires a goal.

I will . . . what? What have you promised to do?

Heavenly Father has provided this structure to all of us in the sacred covenants we make within the temple. The honoring of our covenants is the single-most eternally impactful thing we can offer our children. First, it demonstrates the covenant path working in the daily struggles of our lives. We can show our children how, like a modern-day Liahona, a conviction to revealed covenant priorities can lead them through the pitfalls of anxiety, stress, heartache, selfishness, and pride.

Still shot of Lehi teaching Nephi by Book of Mormon Video Production. © By Intellectual Reserve, Inc. Courtesy of The Church of Jesus Christ of Latter-day Saints. Used by permission.

For example, daily interaction with the word of God demonstrates which influences matter the most and provides a comparison to know which influences don't matter at all. Carefully adhering to the law of chastity ensures us of the blessings predicated on that commandment and emphasizes the wisdom in nurturing our relationships. More openly sharing our efforts to repent increases humility and counteracts the divisiveness of pride in our homes.

Our effort to keep our covenants communicates to our children the reality of God in our lives. We sometimes get lost in our daily struggles. It can seem as if we're on a ship in a storm. We are on the bow looking forward and not seeing Christ steering the ship from behind. But even in such a situation, there are answers through our covenants. In a future day we will be amazed to hear of the great power our God has wielded in order to continually teach us truth. I imagine the consistent workings of God in our lives will be made clear to us.

Several months ago, I was working with our ward missionaries to offer support to a young woman as she was learning the gospel. Though this young woman had grown up in a dedicated Christian home, she was learning truths she had never heard before. She was hesitant to commit to a new idea of who God was and what God wanted from her. She had so many questions, which was good, but she felt overwhelmed.

I told her it was okay to not understand everything right now. I encouraged her to take time to focus on how she felt and to work through her questions one at a time. I took the opportunity to testify that as I had studied the gospel, my questions had been answered enough for me to be fully committed. She said it brought her comfort to know that what she was studying *could* make sense.

As parents, we need to encourage our children to ask us questions—and we need to take their questions seriously. When possible, we need to testify that our time studying our own questions has led to commitment. We should talk about some of the questions we have had and how they were answered sufficiently. When we do so, our children can believe that the process of revelation leads to commitment.

Commitment to God leads us to keep our covenants. Covenants are two-way promises with our Creator, linking our mortal actions with our immortal progress. When Nephi committed by saying, "I will," he understood that his physical actions would lead to profound spiritual blessings. Our youth need to better understand this transcendent connection.

How do we show that we honor our covenants? If we want our youth to recognize the power of making and keeping covenants, they need to see that our covenants inspire changes in our character. Is it evident to your children that your covenants are changing your character?

When we follow through on what we have covenanted and more fully and specifically discuss the long-lasting rewards of doing so, our youth can gain a deeper respect for the power that comes with keeping our covenants.

If you need to be more compassionate, explain to your children how the teachings in the temple help you understand that each child of God has supreme value. If you need more unity in your home, explain how the sacred prayers uttered in the temple represent a powerful, unified petition on behalf of specific individuals. If your child feels life is unfair, explain the great joy Adam and Eve felt in the Garden of Eden when they were taught that a Savior could provide a way back to God's presence.

Help your children understand that life's struggles are put in context within the temple experience. Apply your enhanced knowledge of the plan of salvation taught within those sacred walls to your situation. Include your children in this study in any way possible.

Of course, some teachings in the temple must remain sacred. Knowing these truths is the reward for temple commitment and obedience, and they should be given only by God. However, there is a wealth of perspective taught in the temple that can be shared with youth in reverence and with respect. Children are better able to keep their goal of entering the temple when they can feel adoration from God, rather than exclusion, whenever we discuss the temple.

I remember when I learned that my temple recommend was lovingly granted by my Lord as a passport to enduring peace. Our family was on unstable ground financially. We'd had some significant medical expenses from a recent birth at a time when the economy was slowing down, and we were aggressively looking for ways to save money.

Rationalization began to set in. We would be following the direction of our prophet by paying down our medical debt, right? Did I need to pay my tithing and the interest payments on that medical debt at the same time? I decided that, no, I did not. Did I pray about it? I did not.

I tried it for several months. Not only did our financial situation not improve, it got worse. I began to question my choice, and the obvious became obvious enough for me to recognize it, even in my stressed-out mental state. We sold our second car and began paying a full tithe once again.

I biked, pulled, and trekked our three little girls everywhere I needed to go, rain or shine, all over town. The resulting blessings came in the form of dedicated friends who made the process easier, my children not revolting while riding in the rain, and the physical strength to climb the long slope to the church.

Did my debt go away? Yes and no. It was paid down more quickly than I had imagined but not as quickly as I would have preferred. There was no oversized check in the mail in response to my obedience.

Nonetheless, the debt was paid off. Sometimes simply surviving is the often-overlooked proof of Godly support.

However, I do specifically remember one instance shortly thereafter. My family and I were all together sharing a family joke, and I was full of silly joy. I asked rhetorically, *Lord, why am I so blessed?* The answer came unbidden: "Because you paid your tithing." At that moment, I felt a deep indebtedness to my Savior—one I will never be able to repay. He had provided me with so much more than I had sacrificed for Him, my cherished family being just the beginning of a long list.

At that time in my life, I could have made a wish list: a four-bedroom house, a college degree, a vacation to a foreign place, and financial security. However, I came to realize that in being obedient to the law of tithing, I was opening the door to temple covenants and blessings. My Savior had already prepared His home for me. The Lord was admitting me to His university to learn pure knowledge. He wants to guide me in seeing wondrous sights as He sees them. I can feel secure in knowing He sees *me* as wondrous.

As a parent, I needed to share this experience, all of it—my failings, my repentance, my answer from the Holy Ghost, and my increased appreciation for the temple—with my children, leaving nothing out. To fully understand the blessings of repentance and the depth of progress that can be made, children need to see the full process. This is how I can testify to my children of "the dealings of that God who had created them" (1 Nephi 2:12).

In March 2020, President Nelson sent an email in honor of the First Vision bicentennial year. In it, he reminded us, "In the scriptures there are very few instances in which the voice of God the Father has been heard. So, when he says something, we really need to *listen*. Repeatedly, he has introduced His Beloved Son, Jesus Christ, with a specific charge to 'Hear Him.'"[32] How blessed we are to witness the wealth of interactions between Jesus Christ *and* Heavenly Father within our temple experience! Where do we have a better opportunity to "Hear Him" than within His house?

When we make covenants with our Heavenly Father in the temple, He provides all the tools we need to be spiritually resilient. Let me explain some examples of how our saving covenants—including those made in the temple—create the conditions for spiritual resilience.

The law of the gospel hinges on the Atonement. Christ's perfect grace compensates for our imperfections. More fully recognizing that our imperfect efforts are needed, appreciated, and accepted can increase our motivation.

Rather than getting down on ourselves when we make mistakes, remember there is almost nothing we do perfectly. Accept it. Thank God for loving us anyway and keep trying. We need to remember that Christ has planned for our limitations and through Him we can overcome our limitations.

Living the law of obedience requires us to cope with the changes and challenges we face within Christ's framework of commandments. Christ's part of this two-way promise guarantees He will not require more from us than we are able to bear.[33] This reassurance should strengthen our resolve to stay true to the commandments. If our struggle is not yet removed it confirms we still have the power we need to continue.

Does this mean everything bad that happens is coordinated or on purpose? No, it does not. But it does mean God knows us, cares about us and is aware of our sincere efforts. He will step in when needed and if needed. We must trust him.

The law of sacrifice teaches us relativity. Since our sacrifices are in similitude of Christ's perfect sacrifice—the benefits of which are all-encompassing and could never be overstated—the law of sacrifice emphasizes that our personal sacrifices are also worth the effort. If Christ's sacrifice was worth the effort, then so are ours.

President Joseph Smith, despite all his visions and angelic tutoring, could not find the words to describe the joy of heaven. President Brigham Young declared he would do nothing to jeopardize his place beside his Savior. Joseph F. Smith taught us how we do not belong in this world but will someday go home to God and be in our real home. The Plan of Salvation teaches us there is a joyful place customized for each one of God's children. Our temple covenant of sacrifice promises us it will be worth the effort to get there.

The law of chastity is needed to preserve our virtue, purity, and focus. In connection with the gift of the Holy Ghost, it ensures we can be a receptacle of divine communication and discernment. Thus, we are more capable and effective than we would be otherwise. The law of chastity brings us as close as is humanly possible to the same power that created the world and everything that is in it. By staying focused on the power Christ wants to give us, our effectiveness and joyfulness can only grow exponentially.

Living the law of consecration empowers us to do more than we could alone. This binding contract secures all Christ can give us in exchange for all we can give Him. It offers the promise of unity and collective support from God and our fellow members sharing our load among many. It requires our willingness to recognize the value in others, the same way Christ recognizes the value in us. It is the promise of answers customized to our situation and solutions customized to our needs.

I worry that our youth do not realize how much the law of consecration will be a guiding force in their future lives. They need to learn a broader application of the law of consecration. When Christ teaches his most memorable lessons of "love one another" (John 13: 34–35) or "have no disputations among you" (3 Nephi 11:28) or "be one" (Doctrine and Covenants 38:27) it is because his great store of revelations and endowments are predicated on our ability to be unified. This unification will bring greater ability to overcome lingering problems of the past and challenges of the future.

Our sealing promise guarantees rewards as everlasting as our efforts. Our daily choices to cherish and honor our partner lead to a cherished role of honor with our Father. Our sealing covenant gives a closer understanding of our future roles and a better appreciation of how we must practice these roles now.

We can be more confident in our choices knowing our careful reliance on the Holy Ghost will not lead us astray. Knowing what is fact, discerning what is right, protecting those we love, and knowing what is to come are benefits promised and possible, based on our obedience.

Being endowed with the priesthood—Christ's power—proves He intends for us to be useful and purposeful. The continual work we do with these endowments must be effectual, or He would not have provided us with such a powerful tool. All these covenant truths work together to give us every reason to have a firm spiritual resilience.

President Nelson made an exciting prophecy at the dedication of the Rome Italy Temple in March 2019.[34] He said the opening of the temple in Rome marked "a hinge point in the history of the Church." He also said, "Things are going to move forward at an accelerated pace. The Church is going to have an unprecedented future, unparalleled. We're just building up to what's ahead now." It is no coincidence this statement was made in the shadow of one of the Lord's houses. It is there that we gain the power to make "unprecedented" and "unparalleled" strides.

What promises have you made in the temple? What do you hope for in return? What questions did you recently consider while sitting in the temple? What insights were you taught? What solutions did you recognize by withdrawing from the outside world?

I encourage you to teach your children why you honor the covenants you have made. Explain why you made them and why you keep them. I encourage you to demonstrate the importance of those covenants by attending the temple often and referencing your covenants more often in your speech at home.

When you are bold, reverent, and honest in sharing these instances of empowerment with your children, they will be able to identify the benefits of their own convictions more clearly. A child is more likely to know he will be blessed by living the gospel if his parents talk about the blessings that flow into their lives because they follow Christ. This is one of the ways spiritual motivation can be fostered in our youth.

We have discussed what we, as adults, have promised to do. What have our youth promised to do? Certainly, it is difficult to say the words "I will" without first understanding "I can." Again, as President Nelson testified, we need to do more to help our youth understand that they "have the capacity to be smarter and wiser and have more impact on the world than any previous generation" (Nelson, 2018). Our youth need more encouragement and a clearer vision of what they can do.

Self-doubt is one of the most widespread threats to the spiritual growth of youth today. It blurs vision and prevents progress. I have seen children self-impose imaginary barriers on themselves for unsubstantial reasons, stopping them from doing something bold and good. "You just don't do that." "That would be weird." "No one talks like that." "I can't just go talk to them." In extreme cases, I have seen youth cower rather than speak up when they have a question. I have seen youth hurt themselves because they doubt their worth.

How can we address these widespread concerns when the youth are meant for such great work? We have been advised to allow youth to serve in more leadership capacities.[35] We need to take that seriously if we want to combat self-doubt in our youth.

Supporting youth leadership must be a priority for parents as much as for youth leaders. Youth leadership has been established within our Church organizations to help youth know they have what it takes to make smaller commitments, which can eventually lead to ever-larger commitments.

The 2020 general conference of the Church included two youth speakers. What a powerful message for the youth of the Church. When one youth sees another youth lead out, it immediately reinforces how capable they all can be. It immediately shows how self-imposed barriers that block actions and relationships may not be necessary after all. Seeing other youth lead can provide a relevant example of actionable options they may not have considered before.

The gap that occurs in a child growing to a teenager or a teenager growing to an adult can seem like a chasm for some, creating doubt where an "I will" is needed. Allowing children more responsibility helps them see more clearly that they are capable of taking the next steps on the covenant path.

In my calling leading youth, I have fallen into the trap of making a plan, then handing over an agenda for a teenager to read and calling that "youth leadership." That kind of thing doesn't make youth feel more capable or impactful. In fact, it can make them feel like their leadership role is just for show.

Youth leadership requires that parents and adult leaders integrate adolescents more fully into leadership decisions, planning processes, and adult meetings at home and at church. We must seek input from youth earlier—not after a decision is mostly made but while the discussion is in its beginning stages. They must be given time to consider their opinions and develop ideas. Young people must also be given a chance to contemplate the ramifications of a decision.

The following are some ways you can help youth develop leadership skills at home and in your ward. These practices can build their confidence in seeking spiritual guidance and motivate them to continue in Church participation.

- Give youth a more active part in family councils. Make these councils an important part of your family unit.

- Assign them to help another family member with a special homework project, in practicing a sport, or in reaching a goal.

- More often include quorum and class presidents in adult presidency discussions at the ward level and youth committee members at the stake level.

- On behalf of ward councils, ask for youth presentations on specific topics or upcoming events.

- Create youth committees to participate in the planning of extended family, ward, and stake events.

Most importantly, leading youth requires that we place more value on what they say to us rather than what they hear from us. We need to listen more than talk. We need to ask more than answer. Both teachers and parents need to quietly give the youth plenty of opportunities to share their opinions and insights. When they are unwilling to talk, ask different questions till you find the topic and/or tone that motivates communication.

Another place where our youth can find opportunities to commit to an "I will" mindset is within the home-based learning programs the Church has instituted. Home-based learning is the perfect environment for youth to feel more comfortable participating in personally relevant discussions. Do not assume you should ask easier questions; ask deeper ones. Do not assume the youth have nothing to say; ask them for their input. Let them teach.

Our youth are wise, insightful, empathetic, and capable. Wanting to make an impact is one of the defining characteristics of their generation. We need to help them see what they *can* do so that they can commit to what they *will* do.

Chapter Summary

- *Keeping our covenants is the most important example we set before our children.*

- *Talk more frequently about the blessings that come with keeping our covenants.*

- *Our saving covenants create the conditions for spiritual resilience.*

- *Focus on youth leadership in combating self-doubt.*

"I testify that God is our Father. Jesus is the Christ.
His Church has been restored to the earth.
His truth, covenants, and ordinances
enable us to overcome fear and
face the future with faith!"

—RUSSELL M. NELSON[36]

Chapter 7

GO AND DO

What Are You Asked to Go and Do?

"And it came to pass that I, Nephi, said unto my father: I will go and do."

—1 NEPHI 3:7

I LOVE THE WORDS "GO AND DO." They are words of power. They are words of action. Our actions help us to know whether we are progressing or stalling in our spiritual development. I'm referring to actions such as noticing a thought and following through because you recognize the interaction of the Holy Ghost, or implementing a call to action from our prophet because you trust in his foresight, or eagerly searching for your next step, essentially asking, "Lord, what can I do for you?"

Resilience requires flexibility, malleability, and advancement despite opposition—none of these can take place without action. Consider the scripture from Paul:

For we know in part, and we prophesy in part. But when that which is perfect is come, then that which is in part shall be done away. (1 Corinthians 13:9–10)

When we receive "prophecy," or knowledge, from the prophet or the Holy Ghost, we are given a new "part" to consider, each part bringing us a fraction closer to perfection than the last. Spiritual resilience means integrating each new part as it comes, changing our perspective and thereby our choices and actions.

Lehi exemplifies this dedicated flexibility here:

And it came to pass that the Lord commanded my father, even in a dream, that he should take his family and depart into the wilderness. And it came to pass that he was obedient unto the word of the Lord, wherefore he did as the Lord commanded him. (1 Nephi 2:2–3)

Lehi was told he and his family were in danger. This would change his life forever, yet he did not hesitate to act accordingly. As we face temporal changes or gain further spiritual revelation, we see life from a new perspective. We must adapt accordingly. If that new perspective consistently brings us closer to our Heavenly Father, then we have taken another step in building spiritual resilience. Spiritual resilience required a willingness to give up our comfortable and familiar routines, even the good ones, for something closer to perfection.

The announcement of Children and Youth required me to adapt. I had to take some time to recalibrate my understanding of how to be successful in my calling and my parenting. I realized that we had graduated to a new stage in our development. As a collective Church, we were ready for our next steps, and I celebrated. I came to recognize how the revealed guidance was going to lead us to more effective results at a quicker pace, and I wanted to integrate it in a way that would work for my family.

I asked the Lord what would be my best first step and was a little surprised to learn that I personally should take it slow. Nevertheless, I have been listening each time He gives me further direction. This recalibration and integration process is necessary every time we take a step in developing spiritual resilience.

Hearing the Spirit testify that a gospel principle should be followed is a gift, but is only the first step. The follow-up action is what gives a principle strength and adds to our resiliency.

Consider these examples. You can learn about chastity, but unless it leads you to eliminate inappropriate influences in your home, it did not reach its intended goal. You can hear "love thy neighbor," but unless it stops you from shrieking at an ungrateful, disobedient teenager, it was not as useful as it could be. You can be ordained with the priesthood, but unless you are praying to know how to use the priesthood, some of its effectiveness to serve the people around you is lost.

Going and doing brings tangibility to our faith in a way our children cannot otherwise perceive. Our youth need to know that the covenant path works, even if there is no physical iron rod to hold on to. There is no Liahona to hold in our hands. We must look for guidance in the scriptures and through our prophets, but gospel principles become most evident in our actions—actions backed up with the knowledge of *why* we act.

Nephi's father directed him to leave their camp, travel several days back to Jerusalem, and obtain the valuable plates of brass from Laban. Nephi's response is found in 1 Nephi 3:7. This was a mission fraught with danger, not only because of having to travel a distance through menacing territory, but because obtaining something so valuable from Laban would be difficult. But that's not all: Nephi was already in the middle of a challenge when he committed to "go and do."

Nephi did not voice these memorable words while sitting on a cushion in his father's beautiful house. He did not say them while surrounded by like-minded friends or while safe, well fed, or well-informed. Indeed, his brothers had murmured because of this "hard thing" (1 Nephi 3:4) that was required of them.

Nephi was completely homeless, had few resources, constantly struggled with his volatile brothers, and was under the stress of knowing that all his former friends, extended family, and acquaintances would be conquered. Unaware of how he would accomplish yet another impossible task, his options on how to proceed were limited. Yet he knew it was the Lord who had "required it of them" (1 Nephi 3:5).

How did he know what to do? First, he relied on his brothers and luck as they "cast lots" (1 Nephi 3:11) to decide who would approach Laban. That didn't end well. They then attempted to use their "precious things" from "the land of their inheritance" (1 Nephi 3:22) to purchase the plates. That was also unsuccessful.

But do not assume that these first two attempts were failures. They provided the context that clarified the best path; they were part of the process. Each attempt stripped away a "crutch" Nephi thought he needed to be successful. Identifying these crutches helped Nephi understand where not to place his trust during future challenges. Never again would he rely on his brothers for leadership or complain about his lack of resources.

Because of these challenges, Nephi was forced on his third attempt to walk forward solely on the strong legs of faith, relying only on Christ. Nephi had no other option if he intended to hold true to his promised "I will." Miraculously, it was his *limited* options that ultimately led to his success. Nephi, Sam, and especially his faithless brothers were forced to focus on the only path forward: trusting Christ—a lesson critical to their future progress.

We also need to remove the crutches we use in our own lives and rely more fully on Christ and the guidance of the Holy Ghost. Crutches are used for support, but they are appropriate only if we don't already have legs that work. Consider for a moment how odd it would be if everyone who had strong legs walked around with crutches. Why would anyone use crutches when it would be much more efficient to simply walk? After Nephi's crutches were removed, he "went forth" (1 Nephi 4:5) on possibly nervous but moving legs. He was led by Christ and found success.

On what crutches do you rely? Are there crutches you feel are necessary for your success? What do you feel is more necessary than following the prophet's direction? Have you asked the Holy Ghost about why you feel that is more necessary?

Relying on our comforts to prove we are blessed is a crutch. Waiting for a more convenient time to act on a prompting is a crutch. Discussing our principles only when we feel comfortable is a crutch. Habitually scrolling through our phones to fill time is a crutch. Assuming our children's future success depends on a process we can schedule, purchase, or plan is a crutch. Needing a time-consuming lesson plan to feel like a successful teacher is a crutch. Waiting until our spouse can go to the temple with us is a crutch. Using family prayer as our primary communication with God is a crutch. Assuming seminary will teach our children the scriptures is a crutch. Relying on someone else's answers, rather than seeking the Holy Ghost, is a crutch. Neglecting to pray for direction or confirmation because a decision seems reasonable is a crutch.

Our children need us to drop the crutches that are slowing us down and obscuring our testimonies. Our children need to see our actions even more than they need to hear our words. We are at a turning point in history. Revelations are coming quickly. We need to keep up. Divisions are growing wider. We need to be responsive.

Our commitment to the gospel must show more clearly in our daily actions. Improving our commitment to Christ and acting on that commitment will do more to build the spiritual resiliency of our youth than any of our other endeavors.

How Can Youth Best Learn the Gospel?

When it comes to building the testimonies of our youth, consistent, faith-filled opportunities to demonstrate the relevance of the gospel in the home are much more effective than the Young Women or Young Men programs, Primary, Sunday School, or Seminary. Our teachers and leaders are dedicated, inspired, and authorized in their roles. They are guided to teach foundational principles and to provide a platform for shared experience for the class as a whole. They cannot, however, replace the consistent, private, comfortable, intuitive role of parents.

Parents can explain a doctrine and then demonstrate it in their daily actions. Doctrine can become much more relevant when children can ask a question and see the answer reflected in their parents' choices or hear how it applies to a current family circumstance. Church programs truly support the work of building testimonies, but our homes must become the primary source of gospel instruction. Our homes are where spiritual resilience is fostered.

If *action* sounds like nothing more than work and time, don't stress. We do not need to do everything, but we can do a little more than we're currently doing. In some cases it might be to let go of something time-consuming so you can make room for something more effective and less stressful. Our goal needs to simply be to progress from where we are to where we want to be at the pace and in the direction the Holy Ghost dictates.

Our to-do lists as parents seem to get longer with each passing general conference. Please don't let that overwhelm or discourage you. Feelings of inadequacy can chase away the benefits of stewardship and guidance. It is very difficult to feel empowered through the Holy Ghost when we are constantly reminding ourselves we are not good enough.[37] If you need some reassurance on whether your efforts are acceptable for today, ask in prayer and write down the response you receive.

You don't need to integrate every program in an ideal way from the beginning. The ideal way forward for your family each week or each month is to do what the Holy Ghost advises within the revealed framework. The point is for us to focus on the goals taught by our prophet and move continually forward. How grateful I am for a new, inspired vision designed to bring each of us closer to our most helpful friends, Jesus Christ and the Holy Ghost. Set a goal you can reach, reach that goal, then repeat.

It doesn't matter where you start. Your progress is measured by your actions. As you more thoughtfully and purposely turn your actions toward your Savior, the change in you becomes obvious. Your children need to see greater commitment from you. Children who believe their parents are trying to follow Christ are positively impacted whether their parents are just beginning or . . . well, let's be honest—we're all in the beginning stages relative to Christ!

I love the scripture that says: "And why call ye me, Lord, Lord, and do not the things which I say?" (Luke 6:46) If we ask for Christ's help, we should do exactly what He tells us to "go and do." It's the most effective way to reach our highest goals. Christ has asked us to read the scriptures in our homes daily; this has been emphasized in *Come, Follow Me*. He has asked us to care for the people around us; this has been emphasized in the ministering program. He has asked us to personally seek His direction; this has been emphasized in the goal-focused Children and Youth program. He has asked us to attend the temple regularly; this has been emphasized by the multiplicity of temples being built around the world.

Christ has given us direction on what He would like us to "go and do." He has also given our children direction on what He would like them to "go and do." How do we and our children build motivation to do what He has commanded? How do we keep track of all we are asked to do?

We start with where we are and prayerfully ponder precisely what the next best step should be. Then we build from there, following the direction of the Holy Ghost. Christ is the teacher and grader; the Holy Ghost is our tutor. We and our children can receive customized direction for every type of situation, at the exact time needed, for our next step forward. Then we have to trust that the direction given is sufficient for now. This last part is sometimes the hardest.

We must also recognize that the Savior *loves* our children. I can honestly say I try very hard to do what Christ has asked of me—and if there is something I am capable of doing that would help my children, I believe my Savior will tell me. Sometimes children won't listen to our direction. Sometimes we are not capable of doing all the right things. Therefore, we need to rely on the plan—Christ's plan—because He's prepared for both of those scenarios. Go and do what you can, when you are directed, and trust the Savior with the rest.

I recently asked the Young Women in my stake a series of questions to gain some insight on whether they felt capable of following the doctrine of Christ. Some of their answers were quite funny, though hopefully sincere. I started by asking them, "What do you think the Lord wants from you right now?" Here is a selection of their answers:

- No pre-marriage handholding!

- Love one another

- Be kind

- Have a willing heart

- Have empathy

- Testimony

- Be an example of Jesus Christ

- Share the gospel

- Do my very best

- Keep following the commandments

These answers—often referenced in Church materials—represent important goals, yet they are broad and generalized and include no specifics as to the way to reach these goals. The path from where they are to where they want to go is not so clear. I think most adults would answer in similar ways.

Could it be that the reference to the Lord within the question signaled to the girls that they should respond with answers that felt bigger and more scripturally supported than with something that felt more manageable and personally relevant?

Another, almost identical question focused on them: *Goal setting doesn't mean trying to be perfect. What do you feel prompted to change first?* Some of their responses were:

- Going to the temple more often

- Being nicer to my siblings

- Putting myself out there; I'm too shy

- Better using my free time

- Improving my attitude in the mornings

- Reading my scriptures more often

- Calming my stress

- Improving my diet

- Being a better runner

- Improving my outlook on school

- My glutes!

- Finding my motivations

These answers were much more specific. When referencing "the Lord," their aspirations were lofty—but when focused on personal improvement, their goals were manageable. Why were smaller, more specific answers not given to the question about what the Lord wanted? Could it be the girls did not truly believe that small, incremental progress is good enough for the Lord? Do you know that your small, daily efforts are good enough for your Father?

Any committed, Spirit-led effort is acceptable to the Lord. Always! He knows more than anyone does that small, personalized goals are more effective at creating change than unrealized, grand plans. Our efforts to come closer to our Heavenly Father and Jesus Christ are always good enough, when righteous intentions prevail. The youth need to understand that better progress can be made by selecting smaller, specific goals rather than those that are grand and vague. Set the example and talk about what you are doing.

You can be sure your family life is improving in the fastest way possible when you are going and doing as the Holy Ghost directs.

Ask the Holy Ghost, "What should I do today?" Then wait for His answer. What is the Holy Ghost asking you to do first?

Christ created the earth and all that is in it. At the beginning of each day He received direction from His Father on how to do so. He carried out His task one day at a time. He was never in doubt that His direction came from God. He never doubted the wisdom or sequence of the direction He was given. He did not assume the task was greater than what He could complete, nor should we.

CHAPTER SUMMARY

- *When we show our faith through our actions, we give our children a clear example to follow.*

- *We must let go of the crutches slowing down our spiritual progress.*

- *The home is the best place for youth to learn the gospel and develop resilient testimonies.*

- *Acknowledge the recent flood of revealed adjustments as direction on what God wants from us.*

- *Our small but consistent efforts are always acceptable to the Lord.*

"To know isn't enough. The devils know and tremble;
the devils know everything.
We have to do something."

—SPENCER W. KIMBALL[38]

....
....
....
....
....
....
....
....
....
....
....
....
....
....
....
....
....
....
....
....

Still shot of Laman, Lemuel, Sam, and Nephi by Book of Mormon Video Production. ©
By Intellectual Reserve, Inc. Courtesy of The Church of Jesus Christ of Latter-day Saints.
Used by permission.

Chapter 8

FOR I KNOW

Why Do You Follow Christ?

"And it came to pass that I, Nephi, said unto my father: I will go and do the things which the Lord hath commanded, for I know . . ."

—1 NEPHI 3:7

WITH THE PHRASE "FOR I KNOW," Nephi is telling us he has a "why." In other words, he knows why he is willing to do what the Lord has commanded. It is not simply because the Lord has asked it of him; there is a deeper truth resonating within Nephi, one important enough to motivate him to push comfort, personal preferences, and safety aside. He knows there is a way forward and that Christ will show it to him.

Perhaps one of Nephi's greatest desires—one of his "whys"—was to develop a connection with Christ. Perhaps he wanted to experience again the joy of when Christ "did visit" him (1 Nephi 2:16). He sought progress, knowing Christ would manifest Himself along the way. Understanding why he was willing to act was the element of Nephi's testimony that compelled and inspired him.

What is it you want the very most? Why should you do what God tells you to do? There are things we want for our children, such as attend college, serve a mission, marry in the temple, get a job, be a good parent or spouse, obey the commandments, live in the celestial kingdom, and receive exaltation. We want these things for ourselves. We need to dig deeper to determine *why* we want these things. Only when we determine the why are we able to truly see the direct connection between Christ's plan and our happiness. It is only through Christ that we can receive what we genuinely want most.

Everyone has his or her own whys, but let's look at one example of uncovering the why hidden under a "what": get good grades. I often hear youth use homework as an excuse for not reading the scriptures; their homework needs to be done so they can get good grades. Why would someone want good grades? Because it leads to college. Why does someone want to go to college? Because it can lead to financial security. Why does someone want financial security? To avoid being trapped with limitations. Why does someone want to avoid limitations? Because he or she wants freedom. There it is: the real motivation!

The above exercise demonstrates that there is a reasonable connection between homework and freedom. Christ provides the truest form of freedom. Only He provides a guarantee of eternal freedom, whereas homework provides the possibility of temporal freedom. He is the only one who has the power to control the forces that limit us and are truly outside our control. Even though we may feel like other things are more pressing, time spent in the scriptures provides access to the highest source of freedom.

Once we know what we want most, we can study it, make connections to it in family lessons, show examples of how Christ offers it, and identify better ways to achieve it. But we can't know the powerful personal impact of teaching the true extent of the freedom Christ offers until we uncover what we want the most.

Our personal why will foster in us the hope required to build spiritual resilience. It will help clarify what we risk when we put family-centered gospel learning on the back burner. Our secular goals may be important, worthwhile, and inspired, but too often our spiritual goals receive too small a portion of our daily attention. While doing homework may be important, it cannot compare to the rewards and security of building the spiritual resilience that leads to eternal freedom.

What is it you want the most: truth, comfort, ability, strength, knowledge, influence, forgiveness, power, family, peace, opportunity, choice, joy? Whatever it is, Christ wants you to have what will bring you lasting fulfillment and joy. He is the access point for each of these to a degree so incredibly higher than any other source.

I believe most of our unrighteous actions are based on righteous desires that we attempt to fulfill in unrighteous ways outside of the boundaries Christ has taught. It is when we attempt to get what we want most from a secondary, lesser, or quicker source than Christ that we get off track. Christ has provided us with commandments, prophecies, and guidance to ensure that we each can receive everything necessary for fulfillment and joyfulness.

What are you willing to do to get what you want the very most? How do you pursue what you want the most? Do you see the connection between what you want and what Christ has promised you? Are you willing to follow Christ to get it? With such profound blessings promised, how can obedience or humility be unreasonable or unfair?

You probably have multiple whys that motivate you. They may change often, and that's okay. There are many good whys from which to choose, but some are going to mean more to you than others. As parents, we need to pair what we do with why we do it more often in our speech and thinking. We need to help our children understand the connection between what they want and how Christ will help them get it. When explaining a principle to a nonmember, we need to explain why it matters to us.

The why is often the most important part of communication. Why do you seek after the Spirit? Why do you attend church? Why do you honor the priesthood? Why do you teach the gospel to your children? Why do you remain faithful to Jesus Christ?

It is our whys that bridge the gap between principle and action. Which benefits or promised blessings resonate most with you? What motivates you to go forward? What do you most hope for that makes your spiritual effort worthwhile?

Nephi was willing to go and do. Why? Because he knew God would always lead him to where he needed to go. He would again trek through the desert. Why? Because he knew following the Lord's command was for his benefit. He would again encourage his brothers to be faithful. Why? Because he knew they were part of God's plan. He would build a ship. Why? Because he knew Christ was teaching him. He would sail his family across waters he had never seen, not knowing how long the journey would take or where they would end up. Why? Because his faith was resilient enough to know it would be far better than staying where he was.

I will go and do . . . why? Because I know . . . what? I will follow the prophet . . . why? Because I know he's the Lord's mouthpiece and that in being obedient to my Heavenly Father, I am providing my family and myself My the greatest of blessings. And not only are these blessings for the life to come, but I can enjoy them in quantifiable ways in my life now.

I will integrate the recent Church-wide adjustments. Why? Because I know God will help me navigate the limitations of my personal situation. I will keep my covenants. Why? Because they take away my fear. I will teach my children His gospel. Why? Because I know it is the best way for them to experience lasting joy throughout their lives.

My why is knowing our Heavenly Father has a miraculous ability to overcome challenges. It's a power we should never underestimate. He can manipulate two critical, yet opposing, factors: one that represents limitation (justice), and the other that represents progress (mercy). He can retain both these truths while still allowing us, His children, to reap the benefits.

Let me give you a few examples. Our godly Father can uphold both justice and mercy through the Atonement, allowing us to try again and again. We will all die but will still live forever through the Resurrection, allowing us to be with our family. We cannot see God, but we can hear His voice through the Holy Ghost, which allows us to get the revelation we need. We can experience mental and physical trials, yet still receive the grace of Christ, allowing us to have increased capacity. We can all feel gratitude through the plan of salvation even while experiencing hardship, allowing us a firm sense of purpose regardless of our circumstances.

We can fail and still find success; we can sin yet still live with our Heavenly Parents; we can be mortals yet still be destined as gods; we can retain our agency yet still choose obedience; we can wade through any problems while still knowing we are under the stewardship of Jesus Christ and the Holy Ghost.

These paradoxical truths are all attributed to the careful planning and dedicated work of our Heavenly Parents, Jesus Christ, and the

Holy Ghost. Their forms of compromise are without equal. Their ability to change the limitations of our lives and provide solutions that may not seem possible to our human rationale repeats throughout history, as well as in the details of our lives. This knowledge provides us with infinite reasons to obey Them.

I will sacrifice my time to build the kingdom. Why? Because I know lasting joy grows faster through obedience to God than through personal accomplishment. I will forgive those around me. Why? Because I know the Atonement applies to their mistakes as well as mine. I will wait patiently for more revelation regarding my questions. Why? Because I trust the processes of God. I will follow the promptings of the Holy Ghost. Why? Because I know His guidance is exponentially more effective than my own reasoning.

God's power to use seemingly negative circumstances for our good is evident in Nephi's life. His home would be destroyed, yet he would be safe. His father was wealthy, and yet his wealth was not be needed. He was the younger brother, yet he recognized his own favor with God. His family knew not where to go, yet they were provided for and directed. He would see it happen many more times in his life, as is shown throughout the book of Nephi. Most instructively, Nephi's very first testimony hinges on divine support despite their troubles.

> Having seen many afflictions in the course of my days, nevertheless, having been highly favored of the Lord in all my days . . . (1 Nephi 1:1)

Nephi learned from the scriptures of the miraculous power of God to make opposition work in ways beyond our human reasoning. In encouraging his brothers to not give up on their efforts to obtain the plates of Laban, Nephi referenced some of the scriptural insights that

strengthened his testimony. In the face of the unknown, Nephi faithfully repeated the words "Let us go up" and then declared his reasons
why:

> *Let us go up*, and let us be faithful . . . for behold he is mightier than
> all the earth. *Let us go up*; *let us be strong* . . . for he truly spake unto
> the waters . . . and our fathers came through, out of captivity. . . .
> *Let us go up*; the Lord is able to deliver us. (1 Nephi 4:1–3; emphasis
> added)

Even with Nephi's compelling, powerful statement of what he was
willing to do and why he was willing to do it, his wayward brothers were still not enthusiastic about going and doing. They "were yet
wroth, and did still continue to murmur." However, Nephi says, "They
did follow me up until we came without the walls of Jerusalem" (1
Nephi 4:4). I have seen my own sleepy teenagers grudgingly round the
corner on their way to scripture study enough times that I can relate to
this scenario. Happily, after only eleven years of concerted effort, my
daughters' murmuring has subsided considerably. Yes, that is progress!

Even though they didn't know the dealings of God, at least Laman
and Lemuel were willing to be led. If they had followed their brother's
example and determined their own whys about the gospel, perhaps
they could have begun to build more hope—and thereby more faith.

Ensuring our children know what we do because of our faith and
why we do it is an effective way to build motivation. But the best way I
have found to build hope in my children is to help them identify their
whys for living the gospel.

What do our children want most? Do they know a better way to get
it than through Christ? What obstacles might stand in their way? Do
they understand that God can provide the solutions to these problems?

As a very new first-time mom, I wanted more than anything to honorably care for the child I had been blessed with. I had to rely on the Holy Ghost and not solely my rationale to find the best way to do so. We were barely scraping by financially because we strongly felt that I should stay home to care for our baby girl despite the fact that my husband was actively seeking new employment. I felt selfish and temporally unwise for doing so, but it was what the Holy Ghost was telling us to do. It was scary at the time, but I knew it was the right thing to do. I can never deny the support we received, and still receive, from Christ, who makes all things possible.

I felt weak the first time I realized I couldn't afford the diapers I needed. I felt like an incapable mother in the middle of the grocery aisle. I couldn't hold back the tears. I bought what I could, then went home. Once there, as I prayed to know what I could do to prevent this situation from happening again, I learned there was someone more than just "me" in the equation.

Before even finishing my prayer, my visiting teacher showed up at my door with lunch and a package of diapers. I knew then I could hold on a little longer because God had not only provided diapers; more importantly, He had provided me with a reassurance that things would work out if I followed the guidance of the Spirit. The Savior had provided a better solution than I could have provided for myself. It took a few more months of patient struggling before our financial situation improved, but I was now willing to wait.

We have been asked by our leaders to focus more closely on our spiritual education as individuals and as families. Therefore, we must recognize that following this counsel is ultimately intended to bring us and our children closer to those conditions of faithfulness and guidance that will lead to what we want the most.

Poor relationships, time constraints, unwillingness to participate, stress, lack of basic necessities, illness, or separation can all distract us from gospel learning as a family. We need to remember Christ has a way forward specifically for us.

Are we trying to solve our problems without His guidance in doing so? Are we spending enough time seeking direction from Christ, or are we primarily seeking what we want from secondary sources?

Building our relationship with our Heavenly Father, the Savior, and the Holy Ghost should be our priority, with other pursuits fitting in not only *where* possible, but because they will be *more* possible. Not surprisingly, when we focus on what is spiritually important, time seems to expand. We are able to take care of temporal things more efficiently.

This may require cutting back on a hard-won talent if it is impeding our time with Christ. Perhaps making some tough choices or even a leap of faith is necessary to place a stressor or obligation in the Lord's hands. This decision is between you and the Lord.

The Holy Ghost will help you know what adjustments need to be made in your life. And you can rest assured that He has good reasons why we should make these adjustments. Sometimes recognizing the guidance to give something up is easier than following through. Setting better priorities as a family is when that is particularly applicable.

What activities or pursuits might you need to cut out of your life so you can more fully participate in Come, Follow Me? What might be keeping you from being available to hear that important question your teen may ask only once? What do you need to do to be more present in the time you do have with your children?

CHAPTER SUMMARY

- *Christ is the source for what we want most.*

- *Determining your why creates hope and motivation.*

- *Trust God's powerful ability to problem-solve beyond what you think is possible.*

- *Make inspired changes to your schedule so that doing what the Lord has asked you to do comes first.*

"Please remember this one thing.
If our lives and our faith are centered upon Jesus Christ
and his restored gospel,
nothing can ever go permanently wrong.
On the other hand, if our lives are not centered
on the Savior and his teachings,
no other success can ever be permanently right"

—HOWARD W. HUNTER[39]

Chapter 9

HE SHALL PREPARE A WAY

What Has Christ Prepared for You?

"And it came to pass that I, Nephi, said unto my father: I will go and do the things which the Lord hath commanded, for I know that the Lord giveth no commandments unto the children of men, save he shall prepare a way."

—1 Nephi 3:7

THOUGH NEPHI FACED SIGNIFICANT LIMITATIONS, Christ was ready to help him move beyond those limitations. Nephi had shared with his father his commitment to valiantly follow the Lord, even though he had no understanding of what would transpire over the next few days. He simply packed the things he would need, gathered his brothers, and set off on a three-day journey to the place where his safety had been threatened. He did not know Laban would cheat and threaten him; he did not know his brothers would beat him; and he did not know that an angel would appear to defend him.[40]

Because the Savior had provided a way for Nephi to accomplish that which he had been commanded thus far, Nephi was willing to move forward. Perhaps the angel was sent to reassure Nephi of his mission as much as to reprimand his brothers.

Nephi wrote, "And I was led by the Spirit, not knowing beforehand the things which I should do" (1 Nephi 4:6).

Nephi had been faithful; he learned to trust the guidance of the Spirit. And then he found Laban drunk in the street; God's miraculous solution literally lying at his feet. But Nephi certainly did not expect he would be commanded to kill Laban.[41] To modern readers, this passage can be confusing, unnatural, and even appalling. I imagine Nephi may have felt the same way.

Why would God ask this of Nephi? There must have been another way. Do we not ask this same question from time to time: Why has God asked this of me? Why did God change my circumstances? It can seem so unfair. Wouldn't it have been an easy fix for life to work out differently?

This is not the first time Christ has asked something difficult to understand. The removal of Adam and Eve from the Garden of Eden[42] may have been confusing to their children. Abraham's command to sacrifice Isaac[43] may have felt unnatural to the Israelites. We know plural marriage[44] shocked both the early Saints and many others in our dispensation.

I have felt similar feelings as I read about each of these instances. Some of you may feel this way currently concerning various Church policies. The organization of the priesthood, policies on same-sex attraction, tithing, chastity, or Church discipline are a few possible examples. Nephi's account offers us an example of how the Holy

Ghost interacted with him to help him better understand what was being asked of him. It shows how Christ prepared Nephi for this specific situation years before he would reach it.

Nephi describes how he "shrunk" upon being "constrained by the Spirit" to kill Laban (1 Nephi 4:10). Did this feel like a betrayal of what Nephi thought he understood? Remember the insight my teenager shared in her sacrament talk? Nephi's lack of understanding did not mean God was wrong.

In 1 Nephi 3:7, Nephi testified that he knew the Lord would prepare a way for him and his brothers to overcome any challenges they might encounter in trying to obtain the plates. How had Christ "prepared" the way for Nephi's situation? How did it help Nephi? Look over the teaching process initiated in Nephi's thoughts by the Holy Ghost as he realized each step of preparation leading up to his critical decision.

And it came to pass that I was *constrained by the Spirit* that I should kill Laban; but I said in my heart: Never at any time have I shed the blood of man. And I shrunk and would that I might not slay him.

And *the Spirit said* unto me again: Behold the Lord hath delivered him into thy hands. Yea, and I also knew that he had sought to take away mine own life; yea, and he would not hearken unto the commandments of the Lord; and he also had taken away our property [Preparation 1].

And it came to pass that *the Spirit said* unto me again: Slay him, for the Lord hath delivered him into thy hands [Preparation 2];

Behold the Lord slayeth the wicked to bring forth his righteous purposes. It is better that one man should perish than that a nation should dwindle and perish in unbelief [Reason].

And now, when I, Nephi, had heard these words, *I remembered* the words of the Lord which he spake unto me in the wilderness, saying that: Inasmuch as thy seed shall keep my commandments, they shall prosper in the land of promise [Preparation 3].

Yea, and *I also thought* that they could not keep the commandments of the Lord according to the law of Moses, save they should have the law.

And I also knew that the law was engraven upon the plates of brass [Preparation 4].

And again, *I knew* that the Lord had delivered Laban into my hands for this cause—that I might obtain the records according to his commandments.

Therefore, I did obey the voice of the Spirit, and took Laban by the hair of the head, and I smote off his head with his own sword. (1 Nephi 4:10–18, emphasis added)

The Holy Ghost asked Nephi to do something extreme and confusing but provided clarity Nephi chose to listen to. Our direction from the Holy Ghost is not so difficult to follow. Nephi's directive does not apply to us, but the way the Holy Ghost prepared him does. Even in this shocking trial, the Holy Ghost gave Nephi a reason why he should kill Laban and he also shows Nephi four steps of preparation which helped Nephi understand the why. This preparation was developed over years, yet it is highlighted in Nephi's mind step by step within seconds. It was understanding the whys that helped Nephi make a more difficult decision than we will be asked to make.

Take a look at the four ways in which Nephi was prepared, as noted in the above scripture:

PREPARATION 1. Obeying the Ten Commandments was foundational for Nephi. These commandments developed Nephi's respect of God while simultaneously informing his despair at the thought of killing Laban. His knowledge of those commandments left him feeling torn when he was instructed to kill Laban.

If his preparation had ended here at the basic interpretation of "Thou shalt not kill", Nephi would not have been able to develop a full enough understanding of God and His purposes to obey the command to kill Laban. We should be careful not to stop at the surface understanding of commandments when searching for answers to our own tough questions. The unwritten commandment implied in all others is this: Obey God.[45]

PREPARATION 2. Nephi could not deny the powerful hand of Christ in the events leading up to this fateful moment. He understood this in physically vivid ways through the fear, fatigue, bruises, and awe he'd experienced in the last several hours. Nephi knew that the circumstance he currently found himself in could have come in no other way than through Christ. We, too, need to remember Christ knows our circumstances just as well.

PREPARATION 3. Nephi had developed a love for God's children as a whole. He saw God as the father of many children, not just his own and extended family. This love helped Nephi understand that the directive to kill Laban was for the benefit of future generations and the keeping of an eternal covenant. Nephi had a sense that God's directives benefit not only the individual but must fit many; we need that same conviction.

PREPARATION 4. Nephi's knowledge of the scriptures provided him with a perspective of the grand scale of Christ's purposes. He had studied them, pondered them, quoted them, lived them, relied on them many times.[46] He immediately recognized that for others to develop a similar reliance on Christ, they also had to have the scriptures. The scriptures offer us perspective on the grand scale of Christ's power, entreating us to trust Him.

As he contemplated each of the ways Christ had prepared him and the reasons why slaying Laban was necessary, Nephi finally understood why God had commanded him to do it. Though our decisions will not be so severe, Christ still wants us to have peace of mind that we are making the right decisions, especially when those decisions may be tough to make. He may not be able to give us all the information we want right now, but He has similarly prepared us. Keeping the same foundational truths in mind will help us when our faith staggers along a path we do not understand well enough.

- Obey God.

- Recognize Christ is in charge and leading progress.

- Remember that God's plan must fit countless people, not just a few.

- The scriptures give us wisdom to better see Christ's overarching perspective.

Like Nephi, we can be prepared step by step as we seek the answers to our hardest questions until we can recognize how acting in humble obedience is the correct choice. Some will dismiss a spiritual journey as blind obedience because they cannot acknowledge or do not recognize divine interaction. Nephi acknowledges that he was under the stewardship of the Holy Ghost from the beginning, which led to the step-by-step development he needed. We can also be led by the Holy Ghost as we respect the commandments, acknowledge divine direction, act with charity, and study the scriptures.

As the Lord says, "Come now, and let us reason together." (Isaiah 1:18).

Does seeing how the Lord prepared the way for Nephi provide hope for you? Does seeing that pattern of preparation help you better understand any of God's commands? Does confusion surrounding some of the commandments keep you from developing a stronger spiritual resilience? What example do you want to set for our youth to prepare them for unexpected changes their prophet may announce in their day?

As we follow through with what our prophet—and through him, our God—has asked of us, we will be able to obtain the blessings Nephi did: comfort, reassurance, faithfulness, protection, empowerment, gratitude, wisdom, progress, and joy. Nephi didn't have any idea how things were going to work out. Regardless, he had a great deal of hope that they would.

Do you have hope in the gospel? Do your children have hope that the covenant path will work for them? Do you recognize your greatest spiritual desires as a true possibility? In what direction is the Holy Ghost pulling you? What tasks today feel the most necessary for your family to be successful?

If your answers to these questions are "I'm not sure" or "I don't see any options," I understand. Hang in there a little longer. Stay with Christ's plan a little longer. Our general authorities are describing an outpouring of direction from the Savior. We can experience that same outpouring.

One of my whys for being obedient is knowing that God always has our greatest desires in mind when He asks us to obey Him.

I learned this truth at a critical juncture in my life. At the time, I wondered why certain things were unfolding the way they were. I know now that I would not have been able to truly learn and appreciate the lessons within that experience without the careful coordination of each step in the process.

After graduating from high school, I felt work experience was equally as important as education. I wanted to learn from those who were most successful in my chosen field. I wanted to study the most current problems. I wanted experience.

After a term of summer school, I moved to Brooklyn, New York, to be with my older brother and sister. I was lucky enough to land a job working at an exclusive investment firm on Fifth Avenue in Manhattan. I am certain no one knew how young I was! There was a steep learning curve—which was exactly what I wanted. I felt like I was getting ahead faster than I could have hoped. I enjoyed the prestigious environment and rubbing shoulders with the brilliant, ambitious people that surrounded me. The job was entry level, but I was in.

Despite a promotion and pay raise, it only took a few months before I knew something was not right. The Spirit was telling me to go home. The big-city lights held less and less value for me, but why? This was what I had always wanted—better, in fact, than I could have expected. I didn't understand why my opportunity of a lifetime now felt wrong.

Almost to my own surprise, I turned in my notice. Even then, I was offered another raise and a college education and what I had wanted most: opportunity. It was I who'd said no, but it was as if I wasn't the one talking. I didn't know why I was doing it, but I knew it was the right choice.

I arrived home in Arizona the same night my future husband called me up for our first date. We were married within a year, much to my eternal joy and momentary chagrin (I had promised myself I would never marry so young).

I was doubly surprised to learn I would be a mom just after our first anniversary. My life was profoundly different than what I had planned out in my mind as a teenager. There was one month when I struggled with the ghost of what I had wanted and the reality of what I had. I knew every step was the Lord's doing, not mine, but it was as if I was looking at a picture of myself I didn't recognize. I would come to understand the Lord knew me better than I knew myself.

It took five years for the twists and turns of my past to finally make sense. I learned I could no longer have children. What would have happened if I had ignored the divine direction to leave New York? It is unreasonable to assume the three beautiful daughters I currently have would be a possibility any other way. The Holy Ghost stopped me from unknowingly sacrificing what was truly most precious for something I thought I wanted. He prepared a way for me to learn and appreciate what I wanted most: a family.

Christ knew I would want a family more than I would want a career. He knew it even before I knew it. His direction was critical for me to achieve my greatest desire. Now as the twists and turns continue, I trust him to continue to lead me and to lead those I care about to what we all want most. I am now willing to go and do. Why? Because I cannot be more grateful to my Savior, who prepared a path that I would not have found by myself.

There is a way prepared for you to improve your spiritual resilience and a way for you to teach it that fits your individual situation, regardless of whether you are overworked, have young children, have children without faith, or even if you are teaching children who do not live in your home. None of these conditions negates our responsibility, nor do they disable our ability to follow the Spirit. You can customize your teaching style, schedule, and process. Brainstorm with the Holy Ghost and see what can work for you for now.

This book will not offer you a list of specifics on what to do in your family. Following a list may increase confidence but doing what the Holy Ghost directs increases spiritual resilience and effectiveness.

Christ has prepared better ways for you than I can. Come, Follow Me, Children and Youth, *For the Strength of Youth*, ministering, the increased emphasis on temple attendance, family history, youth leadership, and personal revelation are all Christ's preparations. Pick one to give added focus and let it develop into being part of your family culture. Then pick another.

The gospel education in your home should be tailored to you. Lessons should fit your family dynamic and the lessons your family would most benefit from. I am sure Christ knows that this will require individual direction. He is eager to provide that direction. Ask the Holy Ghost what will work best for your family. Expect the direction to be the size of one sustainable step. He will continue to provide the guidance you need to be successful. Nephi received such direction:

> And it came to pass that the Lord spake unto me, saying: Blessed art thou, Nephi, because of thy faith, for thou hast sought me diligently, with lowliness of heart.
>
> And inasmuch as ye shall keep my commandments, ye shall prosper, and shall be led to a land of promise; yea, even a land which I have prepared for you; yea, a land which is choice above all other lands. (1 Nephi 2:19–20)

Christ has promised us a place/a mindset/a purpose that is "choice above all other" alternatives. Our land of promise may take on a more spiritual or emotional form for now, but it is no less real. As you seek Christ, He will lead you toward that custom-fit land of promise. This is the benefit of having the direction of the Holy Ghost. His directions are customized and continual but lead us all to Christ and our own lands of promise.

Chapter Summary

- *Christ wants to counsel with us so we can feel peace in our actions.*

- *Our lack of understanding does not mean we are on the wrong path.*

- *Christ has in mind what we want the most when He gives us direction.*

- *If we live worthy of the guidance of the Holy Ghost and follow His direction, we will not be led astray.*

"Ye cannot cross this great deep save I prepare [a way for] you
against the waves of the sea, and the winds which have gone forth,
and the floods which shall come."

—Jesus Christ to the brother of Jared[47]

Still shot of Sariah praying by Book of Mormon Video Production. © By Intellectual Reserve, Inc. Courtesy of The Church of Jesus Christ of Latter-day Saints. Used by permission.

Chapter 10

THAT THEY MAY ACCOMPLISH

How Can You Recognize Spiritual Direction?

"And it came to pass that I, Nephi, said unto my father: I will go and do the things which the Lord hath commanded, for I know that the Lord giveth no commandments unto the children of men, save he shall prepare a way for them that they may accomplish the thing which he commandeth them."

—1 NEPHI 3:7

IN THIS VERSE Nephi was not simply talking about himself, but about all of us, the "children of men." He was testifying that we *do* have the power to obey prophetic direction. Obedience allows all of us to reach our righteous goals. We all have the power to accomplish our greatest spiritual aspirations.

That sounds lovely . . . but what if you don't know what the Holy Ghost is saying? What if it doesn't feel like you are receiving guidance?

What if you don't know how to interpret what to do next? What if you haven't really felt the Spirit for a long time?

Our Heavenly Father won't leave us to flail around blindly in the dark. He has promised us the peace and confidence that come from personal revelation. And he has given us a flashlight in the form of scriptures and prophets. But our Father won't carry us when we can walk. To do so would leave us with atrophied spiritual muscles and severely handicap us. So we have to develop our personal-revelation muscles.

First, we must not let stress and swirling emotions drown out His voice. Take a breath; drop your expectations and deadlines. Just hear Him. Commit to take whatever small or bold step the Holy Ghost directs.

Church-wide adjustments have been made because Christ wants more interaction with us on a personal level. These changes will help us better leverage His interaction for greater accomplishment. See what hope it can bring. The adjusted Church programs may be just the answer you have been waiting for. Start there and pay close attention to your thoughts and feelings.

Working to improve my participation in Church programs like Come, Follow Me and ministering has increased my capacity to recognize promptings. I have been quite surprised by how often small whispers of direction have come. It makes me wonder how many I previously missed.

We need to recognize the Holy Ghost's reassurances and interactions with us more often. Elder David A. Bednar taught Church educators that we are "living in the gift of the Holy Ghost."[48] This gift is always with us, but we don't always take full advantage of it.

The Holy Ghost is not like the slow cooker in my pantry that I take out only when something needs to be simmered. He is not a tool I have to dig through my mess to find when I need Him. Instead, the gift of His companionship can be a part of my daily existence—and yours as well. The Holy Ghost is always guiding, nudging, highlighting, whispering, warning, and answering. We need to understand that He is present more readily than we may think. He is active in our lives all the time.

I don't believe we give the Holy Ghost enough credit for the ideas we receive. Those wise words, calming thoughts, recognitions of truth, and amazing solutions all come from Him. Christ's gift to us is really that good. Like the greatest Sunday School teacher of all time, the Holy Ghost is preparing our lessons all week, not just on Sundays.

We all receive promptings in multiple, informal, and personal ways. A simple thought might come to me during prayer, even midsentence, or comments made in sacrament meeting might seem particularly applicable to my personal circumstances, or my husband might be prompted to help calm my worry.

There is no "right way" to receive a prompting. That would imply too much separation between us and Christ because not everyone receives revelation in the same way. President Nelson himself cannot offer a specific checklist. He's said, "You won't find this process spelled out in any manual," though he has promised that as we get better at recognizing promptings, they will be "spiritually invigorating."[49] More fully *recognizing* the Holy Ghost has certainly been invigorating to me. What can be more exciting than knowing God is talking to us?

I recognize the Holy Ghost through a sense of excitement and activity; when the Spirit communicates with me, I can see clearly each step that needs to be taken in a certain direction. Others describe the Holy Ghost as a burning sensation in the heart, pure intelligence flooding our minds, and a feeling of peace and calm. The Spirit can communicate with emotion or with logic, with the heart and with the head.

Some have experienced hearing a voice. Sometimes people describe it as a light-bulb moment—a sudden moment of absolute conviction.

Each of these descriptions is very memorable and describes a clear juncture in our path. Though I can testify of each description from some point in my life, I certainly do not experience pure intelligence or a surge of motivation every day. However, the Holy Ghost is still active in my life every day. We need to more fully recognize the smaller interactions embedded into our very existence, habits and thought patterns to understand what a profound and reliable gift the Holy Ghost truly is.

I have heard the Holy Ghost described as a football we reach out to catch. I'm happy to talk football, but that's not how I see the Holy Ghost. Instead of being the football, His work is better represented by the helmet, pads, coaching staff, water boy, referee, and fans in the stands. The Holy Ghost interacts with every player on our team and every aspect of our game.

Our role in our relationship with the Holy Ghost isn't passive. I have spent too much time thinking I'm the receiver waiting to be thrown a Hail Mary pass—and I've spent too little time recognizing that I'm actually the quarterback with my hands on the ball during every play. Think of the football as your testimony and the Holy Ghost as the many people trying to help you progress it down the field one play at a time.

It is true that we decide whether to be on the field. Similarly, we decide whether we will keep our covenants. However, every good coach encourages the players on the team even if they don't want to play that day.

My path forward has recently included various directives from the Holy Ghost, and I'm sure more will come. None of this guidance has been earth-shattering or difficult. In fact, it's made life better. I've felt inspired to better control my sarcasm, more closely align my eating habits to the Word of Wisdom, recognize when family scripture study has lasted too long, include my children in my Church work, and discuss a lesson idea with my husband. These pieces of guidance were meant to help me be more effective at a pace I could manage without stressing me out so much I blocked the Spirit.

On the other hand, it's so frustrating to encounter a problem only to later realize I had the power and knowledge to avoid it. Have you ever had that experience when you think: *why didn't I follow through with that thought? I knew I should. Why didn't I take care of that?* It has taken me quite a while to recognize that those reminders were prompted by the Holy Ghost.

Even smaller ideas have popped into my head as well: read this scripture, ask this question, send this text, avoid this tone, address this worry. I have come to realize that each of these seemingly unrelated directives has been coordinated by the Holy Ghost to improve my capability to teach Christ's gospel to my kids. I list these only to demonstrate how the promptings from the Holy Ghost can be small yet impactful, quiet yet frequent.

Implementing all these promptings at the same time could feel overwhelming. But they didn't feel stressful as I received them because I received them one at a time. The promptings were presented at just the right moment when I clearly saw a way forward. I was reminded that what was important here was progress, not perfection, and that my loving Savior is ever patient with me.

The hours spent writing this book are a perfect illustration. If I steal away for some quiet time and start writing in a rush without praying for the guidance of the Holy Ghost, I eventually come to a spot where I must simply delete what I've written and start over. The Spirit then reminds me to pray, and the work continues much more efficiently.

This has happened too often! Again, my Savior has been patient with me, focusing on discipline and small, manageable steps toward progress. Indeed, the work dedicated to these words would have been considerably less significant if I could have consistently kept my priorities straight! But I wouldn't have learned what I needed to. Even when I have faltered, He has offered a gentle reminder of "Try again."

I now know following the Holy Ghost is the most helpful, most applicable advice we can ever receive when it comes to succeeding in life. I encourage you to not dismiss those small thoughts, for they relate to your most pressing questions and needs. As a stronger emphasis is placed on teaching in the home, you can expect more detailed direction, which, if followed, will enhance the quality of your life at home. Align your desires with those of the Savior, so improvements can and will be made.

Above all else, this process of developing spiritual resilience has increased my awareness of how all the members of the Godhead work together to support me. My Heavenly Father has created a plan for me, marked with many stepping stones. My Savior offers me grace to expand my capabilities. The Holy Ghost interacts with me through diverse forms of communication, all tailored to my specific needs and circumstances.

However, there are some lessons that require more than a simple reminder. Just because we don't feel the Holy Ghost's warnings doesn't mean we are not being led. There are some lessons we simply cannot fully comprehend except through experiences, setbacks, years of introspection, and extensive hindsight. Because we are under the constant stewardship of the Holy Ghost, and because Christ can fill our needs and our hopes at the same time, all this can be for our benefit.

This is an extension of Heavenly Father's miraculous power to solve problems. We can be busy, challenged, and even take faith-filled risks, but we can be joyful, hopeful, and capable at the same time. We can reserve time as a family and still experience enjoyment and relief from stress. We can focus our time the way the Lord wants us to and be more able to reach our temporal goals, not less. We can face tragedy, doubt, and inadequacy yet still speak with confidence and faith, knowing that our Heavenly Father will help us "accomplish that thing which He hath commanded."

Nephi began with hope and finished with steadfast commitment *because* of his difficult experiences, not *despite* them. When we have spiritual resilience, we can move forward with confidence, even when we don't have every answer, knowing that the Lord is watching over us and having an assurance that eventually we will understand how all of these experiences worked together for our good. Remember, Nephi is writing his testimony many years after the fact. He is looking back and clearly seeing the chronological necessity of this struggle in his growth.

Sariah struggled to understand why she and her family were asked to sacrifice so much.[50] She was worried about being destitute, about her sons' safety, and about being lost in the wilderness. Notice how she testifies that the example of her sons' resilience helped her better understand her own hard experiences:

And she spake, saying: Now I know of a surety that the Lord hath commanded my husband to flee into the wilderness; yea, and I also know of a surety that the Lord hath protected my sons, and delivered them out of the hands of Laban, and given them power whereby they could accomplish the thing which the Lord hath commanded them. And after this manner of language did she speak.

And it came to pass that they did rejoice exceedingly and did offer sacrifice and burnt offerings unto the Lord; and they gave thanks unto the God of Israel. (1 Nephi 5: 8–9)

Sariah and Lehi testify that they gained comfort, reassurance, faith, recognition of protection, added power, joy, and gratitude from the resilience her sons displayed. Likewise, we can be the example of resilience our children need to better understand their hard experiences.

Our hard experiences can teach us incomparable lessons. Read Nephi's words as he recognizes that his trials in getting the plates from Laban were well worth the effort. In the following verses, he acknowledges the wisdom of God and testifies that he obtained what he may have wanted more than all else: progress.

> [We] searched them and found that they were desirable; yea, even of great worth unto us. . . . Wherefore, it was wisdom in the Lord that we should carry them with us, as we journeyed in the wilderness towards the land of promise. (1 Nephi 5: 21–22)

Our hard circumstances can sometimes make us feel like we are living in a box with four thick walls that limit our options and perspectives. We fight against the walls, and many even resent being placed in it. God doesn't want us to stay in the box either. He offers us a ladder in the form of the Holy Ghost and our Savior—an escape over the walls of our box that alters the condition of our reality. We can then pass above the limitations impeding our progress.

> O Lord, wilt thou encircle me around in the robe of thy righteousness!
> O Lord, wilt thou make a way for mine escape before mine enemies!
> Wilt thou make my path straight before me! Wilt thou not place a stumbling block in my way—but that thou wouldst clear my way before me, and hedge not up my way, but the ways of mine enemy. O Lord, I have trusted in thee, and I will trust in thee forever. I will not put my trust in the arm of flesh; for I know that cursed is he that putteth his trust in the arm of flesh. (2 Nephi 4:33–34)

Are there any walls surrounding you that you cannot get over on your own? Are there problems to which you cannot find solutions? As you approach the end of this book, have you gained any insights that apply to your situation? I love the question posed by Elder Bednar: "What did you hear that wasn't said?"[51] What has been triggered in your mind that maybe I have not even written about but that the Holy Ghost has highlighted for your personal situation?

We should give more value to the thoughts or insights triggered in our own minds through our discussions, interactions, and experiences: whispers of thought, comments from others seemingly spoken with a highlighter, a chain of events leading to placing one more puzzle piece into place. All of these are for our good because we are that important to the Lord!

Do not attempt to do more than you are inspired to do at any given time. Maybe the Spirit will tell you to focus on one verse of scripture or one principle at a time. Maybe the Spirit is telling you to first follow through with an action that seems unrelated or difficult but will give you greater spiritual capacity. Maybe you know you are being asked to take a big step. As with any worthwhile goal, we need to take it one step at a time. In doing so, we will know we are capable of obeying whatever the Lord commands us to do.

Sometimes after I pray, or while I am at church, I write the flashes of inspiration or insights that come to my mind, especially in times of stress when my mind is racing a hundred miles an hour and I am unable to focus. How comforting it is to see my paper fill up with varied perspectives of my problem! Not writing down my promptings does not mean I won't receive help; writing them simply helps me be more aware of the help I receive. It is like brainstorming a solution, knowing the Holy Ghost is doing it with me.

I can detect which thoughts are from the Holy Ghost because they are beyond my wisdom. Some thoughts feel so pure it is as if they are written in gold across my consciousness. Others are solid like a rock, weighty and undeniable. Sometimes for a few timeless moments I can reply with a question and receive a response in return, as if I'm in a sacred conversation meant just for me. Then all mixes together again and off I go, focused on what I need to do next.

There have been many times when I was not close to the Spirit, requiring me to honestly reflect on my circumstances. Was my question really ignored or did I dismiss a prompting that seemed too small for my large problem, assuming it must not be the answer? Was the Holy Ghost far from me, or was I frustrated that my answer was not coming at the time I scheduled to receive it? Was keeping my covenants my priority, or did I fill my time with my own solutions? Did I receive an answer, but that answer was "Wait, and rely on the Lord," which felt unsatisfactory for the current circumstance? Did I not receive an answer at all, or had I forgotten the reassurance that I already knew what to do?

Don't assume you are the only one having these feelings. Don't assume your children aren't facing some of the same quandaries. And don't assume your family members, Church leaders, and friends can't help you find answers to these questions through discussions to which the Spirit is invited. Remember how often the Lord has reminded us that if we ask, we will receive. Humbly ask for the assistance your Savior has already made available to you. You are not required to do this on your own. If you include your children in your spiritual process, they will be more likely to include you in theirs.

Our youth want desperately to have successful families and purposeful lives. They want to know they can be capable adults who make a difference. Youth will have more confidence in their ability to make good adult decisions if they know their faith and testimony is helpful when it comes to their parents' decisions. Give them the chance to connect ability with testimony, and they will seek after testimony more often.

We asked our daughters to fast and pray to know how our family should respond to the COVID-19 crisis. They did so and offered suggestions. We gave them spiritual responsibility, and they rose to it. Weeks later, as restrictions began to be lifted, my oldest daughter testified how grateful she was for the guidance of the prophet. I remembered how all her earlier suggestions to me had been centered on the prophet's directions. This is a testimonial bulwark she will continue to build on.

Marriage, family, self-sufficiency, responsibility, influence, testimony, wisdom: these are not only the hopes and dreams of many of our youth, they are also commandments our Savior has given us. Though things may seem impossible at times, I fully believe He will provide a way for *all of us*—His brothers and sisters—to accomplish those things He has commanded us to do.

Christ knows the obstacles facing our youth. He has promised to prepare our youth to overcome those obstacles. To keep this promise, He has given parents a commandment to teach His gospel to their children. He is ready to help each of us in our own situation with our own abilities.

Chapter Summary

- *The Holy Ghost is an active presence in all aspects of our lives.*

- *The Holy Ghost provides guidance that matches our abilities.*

- *Our hope to achieve promised blessings is well placed.*

- *Our success is tied to commandments that Christ has promised to help us obey.*

"May we choose to build up within ourselves a great and powerful faith which will be our most effective defense against the designs of the adversary—a real faith, the kind of faith which will sustain us and will bolster our desire to choose the right.
Without such faith, we go nowhere.
With it, we can accomplish our goals."

—THOMAS S. MONSON[52]

Chapter 11

BLESSED OF THE LORD

How Can the Programs of the Church Make an Impact?

"And it came to pass that when my father had heard these words, he was exceedingly glad, for he knew that I had been blessed of the Lord."

—1 Nephi 3:8

WHAT RELIEF LEHI MUST HAVE FELT knowing that at least one of his sons was willing to take on the role of retrieving the plates. Lehi was not only concerned for his own sons, but also for their sons and their daughters and the children that would come after them. Lehi knew he would not be able to lead them all; at some point, his leadership would pass on to Nephi. Knowing this, Lehi had to let his youthful son learn for himself the workings of his Savior. What a relief for

Lehi to know Nephi had accepted the mysteries of God. No wonder Lehi was "exceedingly glad."

In the period since the new adjustments have been announced by our Church leaders, I have heard many parents describe the home-taught programs as a heavy weight. I can understand why. Yes, we are asked to do a great deal, coupled with a heightened sense of purpose like never before. But our responsibility as parents to teach our children has always been made clear. We have been entrusted with the critical role of teaching those necessary to exponentially further the work of God. He trusts us—and our innovative, independent use of agency—to find relevant, inspiring ways to teach better.

Our youth are described as the "hope of Israel," "children of the promised day," "His most noble spirits," "His finest team," "the youth battalion," "the best the Lord has ever sent," and His "heroes" (Nelson, 2018). Of course, we're going to feel some pressure as we recognize the great responsibility we have been given. Let that pressure seep into your bones and meditate on it for a while! Let that pressure help you understand that you are needed and play a critically important role.

Integrating the new programs and guidance through small steps does not mean we diminish the urgency of following the counsel of President Nelson. We move forward in a spiritually directed, personally customized way as quickly and sustainably as possible. However, small instances of inspiration can create more consistent progress over a shorter amount of time than we may imagine.

A year ago, I did not have any intention of writing a book to support parents in teaching the gospel, but the Holy Ghost is a motivational, transformative force. The change in my focus and urgency came about quickly as I stumbled forward. The steps involved were intrinsically linked to my Church participation and attempts at integrating the recent Church adjustments. I have learned that significant support awaits us as we implement prophetic direction to participate in Church programs.

My change of direction offers the best explanation I can provide of this multi-layered support. Certainly, there is no checklist, timeline, or order that applies to anyone but me in this example. I simply want to demonstrate how the programs of the Church all weave together in surprisingly simple but encouraging ways. We do not need to lift our parental weight alone; we have a lifeline woven from a multitude of strands.

In October 2018, Elder David A. Bednar described our Church support in this way: "Just as a rope obtains its strength from many intertwined individual strands, so the gospel of Jesus Christ provides the greatest perspective of truth and offers the richest blessings as we heed the admonition of Paul to "gather together in one all things in Christ, both which are in heaven, and which are on earth; even in him. (Ephesians 1:10)."[53]

I have witnessed these strands in my life. They are personal and subtle, yet numerous and impactful. I wish to testify of Christ's interaction in my life through His many supportive and guiding strands.

STRAND 1—FOLLOW THE DIRECTION OF THE HOLY GHOST

For a long time—a substantially long time, in fact—I have been taking a few classes every term to finish my college degree. At one point, I was happy to report I had only four more classes before I could graduate, but that was before the day I had the strongest impression to drop my classes. All of them. What?! Why?

"Can I take just three?" *No*, came the definitive answer.

"Two?" *No*.

"How about just one?" *I would rather you didn't, but yes.*
I dropped all but my easiest class.

STRAND 2—ACCEPT CALLINGS

A few days later, I received a new calling. I was thankful to continue working with the youth I cared so much about, but now it would be as a stake Young Women president. Sitting on my couch as I said the words, "Yes, I accept this calling," I *immediately* received a Spirit-led directive: *Focus on building spiritual resilience in the youth.* I thought about that idea and integrated the concept every way I could as I moved into my new calling.

STRAND 3—FOCUS ON THE TEACHINGS OF OUR CURRENT PROPHET AND LEADERS

In confirmation of the directive I had received in accepting the calling, I was guided to Elder Lynn G. Robbins's wonderful *Ensign* article on how to encourage resilience in the youth to better prepare them for the future: "Resilience—Spiritual Armor for Today's Youth."[54] How convenient to find what I needed sitting on a table in my own living room! The Lord truly makes sure that whatever information, knowledge, tools, or resources we need to accomplish His commandments will cross our path at the opportune moment.

STRAND 4—WORK THROUGH CHALLENGES

During my efforts to live up to my new Church responsibilities, almost as if planned, I was asked to speak about building more self-reliance in the youth during stake conference. I fasted, prayed, and pondered on what would get to the root of the topic. What could I say that would be of worthwhile to the valiant, faithful parents of my stake? Through my efforts to gain personal direction, the connection between my love of Nephi's testimony in 1 Nephi 3:7 and my focused study on spiritual resilience began to combine. I began to see how Nephi's experience contains all the necessary principles to develop our own spiritual resilience. Afterward, I began to recognize how many parents desired to understand these building blocks as well.

Strand 5—Go to Church, Read the Scriptures, Say Your Prayers (I know you've heard this before)

Multiple times a week I was given new ideas and insights that directly applied to what I was pondering and studying in the scriptures. Comments in Sunday School, questions from the youth, and topics in sacrament meeting all seemed to support the direction I was being given. I needed to take notes to keep it all straight in my mind.

The same topic came up frequently as I counseled with youth or parents when they described the difficulty of doing their best. Everything came together in a way I could not have clarified on my own. When you commit wholeheartedly to following the Lord's plan, and you press forward in faith, even in the face of challenges, at some point you will find things falling into place almost without effort.

Strand 6—Come, Follow Me

My family and I read the scriptures together the best we know how. I read as many scripture verses as we can while our daughters eat breakfast before running off for early-morning seminary. The ratio between verses, discussion, and Cheerios is in constant flux, but we get to focus on at least some truth most days. We rarely get through every chapter for the week, but we are doing better than we were. There was a time years ago we could hardly read three verses a few times a week. I have come to understand that our collective, continual efforts toward progress are acceptable to the Lord.

I realize this timing may not work for every family, but it does for us mostly because my oldest daughter sets the tone. She rises with the sun and is eternally cheery (except when someone else is wearing the shoes she wants to wear). It is difficult for the rest of us not to be blinded by her early-morning sunshine-like attitude. Her eagerness to learn the gospel has been a deciding factor in our scripture study. She has often used her influence to teach, inspire, and encourage our whole family in significant ways, day after day.

Through these morning discussions and our Awesome Hour lesson on Sunday afternoons, I was taught by my levelheaded husband and through the questions and insights of my daughters. Oftentimes, they'll ask a question and I initially stammer with how ill-prepared I am to answer it. Then the Holy Ghost begins to teach me, and I simply repeat what He says.

STRAND 7—REMEMBER TO BE HUMBLE

The idea of writing a book based on these thoughts had come one varied instance at a time. It was not the same kind of directive I had when I dropped my classes; instead, it was just a simple, repetitive thought. Nervously and hesitantly I started to write, but eventually I had an outline and several chapters.

In December I finished the single class I'd hung on to. I am ashamed to say that as I pined for my lost term I thought, *What was the point of that?* Suddenly, I realized something: I had not registered for my next semester as I had so many times before. Where had my mind been this time? By then, it was too late to register for the few classes I needed. Apparently, our Heavenly Father had His own way of getting my attention—with no backtalk this time!

Strand 8 — Attend the Temple

Time spent sitting in the temple is sacred time; during these moments my mind is calm, and I can listen for the whisperings of the still, small voice. While I pray with my husband, the questions and concerns that fill my mind outside the temple narrow down to only those concerns that are most important. It's as if I get the answer to several questions all at once, without even asking. Sometimes the message is, "Don't worry about those. It will be fine. What do you really want to know?"

Then I can prioritize and get to the temple work not completed by proxy: personal revelation. The temple gives me a greater sense of what I am capable of and what my purpose is, more than any other place.

As I attended the temple, I was encouraged and felt that I was on the right track with my writing. I continued to write with more confidence.

Strand 9 — *Children and Youth*

In January, my youngest daughter informed me that she didn't like the word *goals*. She didn't want to make goals and she didn't want to talk about goals. She said, "If I make a goal, I probably won't finish it. So why am I doing it?" Many young people can probably relate to this sentiment. I am grateful she was honest with me.

To add some context, Ashley is exceptionally resourceful. Her capacity to problem-solve exceeds my own on a regular basis. She is a girl of action, bringing energy and enthusiasm into all parts of her life. She loves learning about the Savior and is beginning to gain a relationship with Him. The problem was not her ability to keep a goal. Instead, what she was really asking was "Why is it important to make these goals?" Or, in other words, "Why can't I just keep doing the good job I am already trying to do?"

We talked about how Children and Youth is not designed for personal improvement by means of setting goals. It's designed to help youth discover what our Heavenly Father wants them to work on. Praying for direction and receiving your task directly from God the Father is not a goal as much as a quest.

We talked about what her first quest might be. She prayed the simplest of prayers. "Dear Heavenly Father, what would you like me to work on first? Amen." Her answer came quite quickly: "Pray more often. I want to talk to you more." She was sure that was the right answer, and then she was the one coming up with the plan. From there, my role was only to act as her scribe. We started with one, then two quests. Once those were well underway, we'd talk about another.

Over the weeks, I received my own weighty inspiration on what to write in this book. My quest was made clear, and it mattered little whether it was for my benefit or for others. My Heavenly Father had asked it of me. This knowledge was quite motivational.

STRAND 10—FAMILY HISTORY

A dear friend came by to give my daughters another lesson on using FamilySearch. It reminded me of people from the past who were given heavy burdens to carry. These people gave their lives to accommodate the direction of the Lord. I've been motivated and inspired by the sacrifices and examples of those who've come before me, including my father and mother and my many great-grandparents. As I've done family history, I've also come to see that not only does our family throughout history help us in many ways with our challenges and quests, but we have another family that we can call on.

A ward family surrounds my husband and I, supporting our efforts to raise our daughters. It is not on my shoulders alone.

STRAND 11—MINISTERING

My wonderful ministering sister came by today. While catching up, she helped me suddenly realize something I had not considered. Our simple conversation helped me answer a question I had been considering for months but did not yet see. What if I were in the middle of a heavy class load right now? I certainly would not have had the time to write during these past months. Maybe our Heavenly Parents' plan for each of us is more detailed than we can clearly see.

I believe the Lord sees our needs and has multiple options to fill them through our ward families.

STRAND 12—TRUST IN GOD'S PROCESS

What was I supposed to do with this book I had been writing? I still didn't know, but I repeatedly had a date in my mind: March 8, March 8, March 8. Okay, I get it—March 8. It spurred me to work much faster than I would have otherwise. Unfortunately, the persistent thought was ineffective at breaking through my own imperfections. By March 1, the manuscript was still not finished.

For me, March 1 to March 8 was packed. That week was my husband's birthday, and I also had four multi-hour Church leadership meetings, in addition to speaking to the stake high-priest quorum.

In addition, I was coordinating an all-day, multiday mission experience for the combined stake youth, during which twenty-five young women would be staying at my house overnight, culminating on March 8, which was a Sunday. I knew I was supposed to submit the manuscript to a publisher, but why that day? Surely, my schedule was no secret to God. The manuscript certainly was not my best work yet, and how could I get it ready by then?

March 8 came and went in a whirlwind. By March 9, I was mentally and physically spent. From March 10 to March 13, I was torn in many different directions. It was my daughter's birthday, our wedding anniversary, our business tax paperwork was due, and a national state of emergency due to the spread of COVID-19 was announced.[55] Irrationally, through all of that, this book still felt like the pressing priority! March 8 was making more and more sense as the news headlines came flooding in. I was pushed to finish the book despite everything else. By March 16, our personal, professional, and church life had been reshaped several different ways, several different times, but the book was written before I could be distracted by the world around me.

I was learning that I did not need to rely solely on my abilities; there is so little I can control, anyway. As piece by piece of our plans were canceled and rescheduled, I was given understanding of an underlying principle. My success could not be lost by a busy schedule, a tight deadline, or an unexpected calamity. My success did not depend on a graduation ceremony; my daughter's success did not depend on an ACT test; my husband's success did not depend on a contract. Each of these could be taken away. As long as these circumstances did not change my obedience to God and my commitment to my covenants, it would not change my access to success. My circumstances are outside my control, but my access to success is squarely within my control. This is a gift envisioned by our Heavenly Father and Jesus Christ.

I have no idea what would have happened if I hadn't pushed to get the book done by March 8, my busiest day of the year so far. But I do know I can trust God in the details of my life. Is that not the whole point of this book? This book can still be improved upon, but my feelings of inadequacy and doubt needed to be set aside, my faith brought to the forefront.

With humility and gratitude, I have listed the strands that have thus far "intertwined" to bring me the "richness" of the blessings offered by Christ. This was a long explanation, but it could have been longer. The support we receive from the restored gospel of Jesus Christ is just that comprehensive. How better can I demonstrate the combined strength of our Church support—coordinated by the Holy Ghost—in the small details of our lives?

Church support is no small thing. Sincerely going and doing as the Spirit directs brings no small benefits. We are not left alone in our teaching responsibilities. Each strand has played a role in a relatively short time in my progress.

We have the support needed to build spiritual resilience despite our questions, limitations, and character flaws. You can rely on a strong safety net woven by these strands within The Church of Jesus Christ of

Latter-day Saints. There is strength in the many guides tugging you in the right direction. Do not resist the opportunities to improve offered by Church programs. Step by step, our Divine Family leads us to solutions, answers, and guidance, starting from where we are to where They would like us to be. All new Church adjustments are designed to strengthen our connection with the divine and to make our safety net more secure. You want more help? God wants to give it to you.

With every past and future revelation, we should remember that we have been deemed ready to receive these revealed adjustments. We have graduated to a new stage in Church history and taken a few more steps toward spiritual progress. We can capably shift to home-taught, Church-supported gospel instruction.

More adjustments will come when we as a collective church are ready for them. I look forward to the coming progress and want to do my part. I welcome the recalibration of my heart and mind that comes with each divinely given revelation. They mark the mileposts of our collective spiritual progress. If Jesus Christ feels our youth are ready for greater purpose and leadership, He certainly feels the same way about us.

In this hopefully helpful book, I have tried to muster all my truth. The Holy Ghost will communicate those things I may not write about but which the Lord wants you to hear. I rely on the grace of my Savior to make up for my lack and yours. Muster your truth. Act on it the best you know how. Look forward with hope, knowing it will lead to progress. Be watchful for the change Christ has prepared for you.

Nephi's spiritual resilience continued to develop through the years, growing stronger with each passing challenge, until it was as solid as a rock. Finally, at the end of his life, his faith would not allow him to move away from Christ. His final testimony, built one day at a time, transcends even the testimony of his youth:

Yea, I know that God will give liberally to him that asketh. Yea, my God will give me, if I ask not amiss; therefore I will lift up my voice unto thee; yea, I will cry unto thee, my God, the rock of my righteousness. Behold, my voice shall forever ascend up unto thee, my rock and mine everlasting God. Amen. (2 Nephi 4:35)

CHAPTER SUMMARY

- *Our youth need independence to learn from the Savior.*

- *Led by the Savior, the Church supports us in discovering what we need to progress.*

- *Revelation will continue; answers are available.*

- *Just like Nephi, all of us can improve.*

"Sometimes we think the whole job is up to us, forgetful that there are loved ones beyond our sight who are thinking about us and our children. We forget that we have a Heavenly Father and a Heavenly Mother who are even more concerned, probably, than our earthly father and mother, and their influences from beyond are constantly working to try to help uswhen we do all we can."

—PRESIDENT HAROLD B. LEE[56]

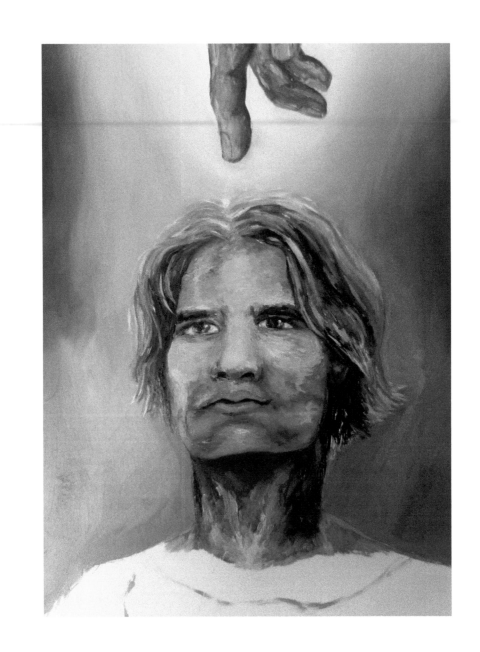

Author's Note

I AM SO GRATEFUL FOR MY DAUGHTER, Evie Goettl, who created a new, modern vision of who Nephi was. Her artistic skill is well practiced and well beyond her years. I had not able to find or create a visual that accurately portrays the person I have been thinking so much about. I should have known a fellow youth would be able to bring him to life in an inspired way.

I want you to see Nephi as a fellow seeker of Christ, full of modern insight and helpful collaboration. I want you to recognize that the source of Nephi's power was Christ's interaction with him and Nephi's desire to work for Christ. I want you to see him imperfect, unfinished, and from a fresh viewpoint.

Nephi's collective experiences colored his outlook with smudges unique to him. Each smear and stain informed his future choices with a valuable perspective that cannot be replicated in someone else. Our unique perspective is also valuable and useful to our Savior.

We are in-process and unfinished. We have gaps in our faith. Our Savior will continue to refine us for our benefit and our families. Refinement is easiest when we willingly participate in change, repent often, and deeply integrate the gospel of Christ.

Acknowledgments

I DID NOT START THIS PROCESS wanting to write a book. I felt compelled to do so. I found something that helped me so I hoped it would help you as well. My hesitancy and feelings of inadequacy have been acknowledged and subsequently ignored by my Savior. "Get to work" was the message continually in my mind. Each paragraph of this book has been prayed over with the words "Please, help me to write something that can be helpful." I need to acknowledge the guidance of my Savior first and foremost. The mistakes within this book are all mine and if even a few sentences resonate with you it is because of His guidance. I only wish I could have been easier for Him to work with. My Savior deserves my utter humility and strongest allegiance.

My parents gave me a firm foundation in the gospel and instilled within me the personal responsibility to learn more. They have given me every motivation and guidance needed to do so. I am grateful for their support as I found and studied the gaps in my gospel understanding until my faith could be as firm as theirs. I thank them for teaching me a confidence that is not based on something as fleeting as what I can control. Instead, my faith and theirs, is based on Christ being in control.

My husband he has been my greatest blessing and is linked to most other cherished blessings. I thank my Heavenly Father for the love of this man. He has heard more about sentence structure, cover design and reader flow than he ever wanted to, but has been supportive from the very beginning. It is due to his care and patience that this book even exists.

At less than half my age, my daughters have learned lessons I am still working on. They can go and do more effectively than I, making me excited for the future. If you feel hope and optimism in my words, it is because my daughters have inspired it.

Dear friends have each taken turns reading the manuscript and making key comments that have improved the finished work dramatically. Camie Sharp and Colleen Gibb have been especially supportive. Thank you for the friendships that have shaped my adult life.

There has been a great deal to learn as a new author. Angela Eschler, Shanda Cotton and the team at Eschler Editing have patiently educated and guided me with expert insight. The editing skills of Kathy Jenkins, Michele Preisendorf, Heidi Brockbank and Cassidy Skousen were oh so necessary and instructive. Each in their turn have improved and clarified the manuscript for greater benefit. These professionals were critical elements of the publication process.

Trina Boice has been a dedicated coach for this new author. Ever encouraging and knowledgeable, she has given me perspective when stressed and insight when stalled. Thank you for helping me reimaging my expectations and feel more confident.

How grateful I am for the artistic skill of others. Scott Eggers took the generous time needed to clarify an artistic direction, as well as help me feel confident when I needed it the most. Erin Seaward-Hiatt has skillfully translated these words into beautiful visuals both on the exterior and interior. The twists and turns of this process were more than one might have predicted. Erin was a resilient warrior, always generous, patient, and skilled.

Creating the audiobook has been a wonderfully insightful experience. Gailen Hegna at Rainbow Recordings provided a comforting space and technical ability as I completed the process of hearing these words out loud for the first time. Thank you for helping them break free from the cramped space within my thoughts.

Throughout the years, the youth leaders I have worked with have each led my faith process, along with the youth we were serving. I have learned from their lessons and testimonies as much as anyone else. Thank you for your dedicated service.

Many youth have gifted me with treasured memories. Utilize your energy and potential to the best of your ability. Thank you for sharing part of your life with me. Thank you for sharing your feelings, testimonies, questions, personal experiences, mutual nights and campfires. Your choices make an impact and I have benefited from them.

Reader's Note

Connect with me at www.sharlagoettl.com and on Facebook @authorsharlagoettl to use "The Goal Maker," a guided questionnaire for creating goals that personally fit you and your family. Want to learn more about my grandfather's journey toward faith? You can find more stories there. I would love to hear any insights you would like to share with me about spiritual resilience.

Posting a review is a great way to ensure this message on building spiritual resilience can reach families who are looking for support.

NOTES

1   The Church of Jesus Christ of Latter-day Saints, *No Unhallowed Hand,* Saints: The Story of the Church of Jesus Christ in the Latter Days (Salt Lake City: The Church of Jesus Christ of Latter-day Saints, 2020), 95. Originally documented in Historian's Office, General Church Minutes, Dec. 27, 1847, 18–19.

2   Russell M. Nelson and Wendy W. Nelson, "Hope of Israel," Worldwide Youth Devotional, June 3, 2018, https://www.churchofjesuschrist.org/ study/broadcasts/worldwide-devotional-for-young-adults/2018/06/ hope-of-israel?lang=eng.

3   Russell M. Nelson, "The Future of the Church: Preparing the World for the Savior's Second Coming," *Ensign*, April 2020, https:// www.churchofjesuschrist.org/study/ensign/2020/04/the-future-of-the-church-preparing-the-world-for-the-saviors-second-coming?lang=eng.

4   Russell M. Nelson, "Revelation for the Church, Revelation for Our Lives," *Ensign*, May 2018, https://www.churchofjesuschrist.org/ study/ensign/2018/05/sunday-morning-session/revelation-for-the-church-revelation-for-our-lives?lang=eng.

5   "What's New in the *Children and Youth* Initiative?" *Children and Youth* webpage, The Church of Jesus Christ of Latter-day Saints, updated January 2020, www.churchofjesuschrist.org/youth/childrenandyouth/ whats-new-in-the-children-and-youth-initiative?lang=eng.

6   "Let Them Lead," Aaronic Priesthood Quorum training webpage, The Church of Jesus Christ of Latter-day Saints, updated June 2018, www.churchofjesuschrist.org/callings/aaronic-priesthood-quorums/ my-calling/leader-instruction/let-them-lead?lang=eng.

7   Neil L. Andersen, "Ministering in a Holier Way," *Ensign*, June 2019, https://www.churchofjesuschrist.org/study/ensign/2019/06/ministering-in-a-holier-way?lang=eng.

8   Ezra Taft Benson, "Listen to a Prophet's Voice," General Conference, October 1972, www.churchofjesuschrist.org/study/general-conference/1972/10/listen-to-a-prophets-voice?lang=eng.

9   1 Nephi 18:22–23.

10   1 Nephi 1:14.

11   1 Nephi 1:20.

12   1 Nephi 8:4, 17–18, 35–38.

13   3 Nephi 10:4–6.

14   Joseph Smith—History 1:25.

15   Joseph Fielding Smith, *Gospel Doctrine: Selections from the Sermons and Writings of Joseph F. Smith, Sixth President of the Church of Jesus Christ of Latter-day Saints*, (Salt Lake City: Deseret Book, 1919), 9–10.

16   Gordon B. Hinckley, "Rise to the Stature of the Divine within You," *Ensign,* November 1989, www.churchofjesuschrist.org/study/ensign/1989/11/rise-to-the-stature-of-the-divine-within-you?lang=eng.

17   Daniel 6.

18   Luke 1:38, 46–55.

19   Mormon 2:2.

20   1 Samuel 17:50.

21   Esther 4:14–16.

22   Genesis 22:9–12.

23   Mark 1:2–8.

24   1 Nephi 12:5–6.

25   2 Nephi 4:20–24.

26   2 Nephi 4:26–29.

27 Moses 7.

28 Aubrey Eyre, "A Look at How Church Leaders Decided on the 2020 Youth Theme and Why It's Important for Youth Worldwide," *Church News*, August 23, 2019, www.thechurchnews.com/ leaders-and-ministry/2019-08-23/a-look-at-how-church-leaders-decided-on-the-2020-youth-theme-and-why-its-important-for-youth-worldwide-157458.

29 Thomas S. Monson, "Be of Good Cheer," *Ensign*, May 2009, https://www.churchofjesuschrist.org/study/ensign/2009/05/be-of-good-cheer?lang=eng.

30 Natalie Goettl, talk given in February 2020. Used by permission.

31 Donald L. Staheli, "Obedience—Life's Great Challenge," *Ensign,* May 1998, https://www.churchofjesuschrist.org/study/ensign/1998/05/obedience-lifes-great-challenge?lang=eng.

32 Russell M. Nelson, "Hear Him," Personal Facebook page of Russell M. Nelson, posted February 25, 2020, www.facebook.com/russell.m.nelson/videos/791321461379415/.

33 A good example of this promise in action is found in D&C 124:49.

34 Sarah Jane Weaver, "President Nelson Calls Rome Temple Dedication a 'Hinge Point' in Church History," *Church News*, March 15, 2019, updated December 27, 2019, https://www.churchofjesuschrist.org/church/news/president-nelson-calls-rome-temple-dedication-a-hinge-point-in-church-history?lang=eng.

35 Young Men General Presidency and Board, "Do You Want to Make a Difference? Let Youth Lead," *Church News*, June 21, 2017, https://www.churchofjesuschrist.org/church/news/do-you-want-to-make-a-difference-let-youth-lead?lang=eng.

36 Russell M. Nelson, "Face the Future with Faith," *Ensign*, May 2011, https://www.churchofjesuschrist.org/study/ensign/2011/05/saturday-afternoon-session/face-the-future-with-faith?lang=eng.

37 Debra Theobald McClendon, "Discerning Your Feelings: Anxiety or the Spirit?" *Ensign*, April 2019, www.churchofjesuschrist.org/study/ensign/2019/04/young-adults/discerning-your-feelings-anxiety-or-the-spirit?lang=eng.

38 "New Verse Is Written for Popular Song," *Church News*, April 1, 1978, p. 16; Joseph Smith Translation—James 2:18–19.

39 Howard W. Hunter, "Worries and Challenges: Fear Not, Little Flock," *BYU Speeches*, 14 (March 1989), speeches.byu.edu/talks/howard-w-hunter/fear-little-flock/.

40 1 Nephi 3:25–29.

41 1 Nephi 4:7–8.

42 Moses 4:29.

43 Genesis 22, Joseph Smith Translation—James 2:20.

44 "Plural Marriage and Families in Early Utah," The Church of Jesus Christ of Latter-day Saints, www.churchofjesuschrist.org/study/manual/gospel-topics/plural-marriage-and-families-in-early-utah?lang=eng; D&C 132: 34–40, 45.

45 Doctrine and Covenants 132:32–37.

46 1 Nephi 19:10, 23.

47 Ether 2:25.

48 David A. Bednar, "What Did You Hear That Was Not Said? Elder Bednar Teaches CES Instructors about the Spirit and Personal Revelation," *Church News*, February 11, 2020, https://www.thechurchnews.com/living-faith/2020-02-11/elder-bednar-ces-broadcast-personal-revelation-174180.

49 Russel M. Nelson, "Spiritual Treasures," *Ensign,* November 2019, https://www.churchofjesuschrist.org/study/ensign/2019/11/36nelson?lang=eng.

50 1 Nephi 5:2–3.

51 David A. Bednar, "What Did You Hear That Was Not Said? Elder Bednar Teaches CES Instructors about the Spirit and Personal Revelation," *Church News*, February 11, 2020, https://www.thechurchnews.com/living-faith/2020-02-11/elder-bednar-ces-broadcast-personal-revelation-174180.

52 Thomas S. Monson, "Choices," *Ensign,* May 2016, https://www.churchofjesuschrist.org/study/ensign/2016/05/sunday-morningsession/choices?lang=eng.

53 David A. Bednar, "Gather Together in One All Things in Christ," *Ensign*, November 2018, https://www.churchofjesuschrist.org/study/ensign/2018/11/saturday-morning-session/gather-together-in-one-all-things-in-christ?lang=eng.

54 Lynn G. Robbins, "Resilience—Spiritual Armor for Today's Youth," *Ensign*, September 2019, https://www.churchofjesuschrist.org/study/ensign/2019/09/resilience-spiritual-armor-for-todays-youth?lang=eng.

55 U.S. President, Proclamation, "Proclamation on Declaring a National Emergency Concerning the Novel Coronavirus Disease (COVID-19) Outbreak" (March 13, 2020): www.whitehouse.gov/presidential-actions/proclamation-declaringnational-emergency-concerning-novel-coronavirus-disease-covid-19-outbreak/.

56 Harold B. Lee, "The Influence and Responsibility of Women," *Relief Society Magazine* 51 (February 1964):85. At this time, Harold B. Lee was serving as a member of the Quorum of the Twelve Apostles and made these remarks during the October general Relief Society meeting; see also David L. Paulsen and Martin Pulido, "'A Mother There': A Survey of Historical Teachings about Mother in Heaven," *BYU Studies* 50, no. 1 (2011): 71–97, first presented at the BYU Studies Symposium 2011.

Photo by Julian McFadden

SHARLA GOETTL has served as a youth leader in The Church of Jesus Christ of Latter-day Saints almost every year of her adult life. Doing so has taught her the faithful capacity of the youth and a respect for the parents who teach them. She currently serves as a stake Young Women president in Oregon.

Sharla is a wife, mother, sister, confidant, instigator, and believer. She listens to the voices in her head, sings loudly out of tune, and dreams of faraway mountains. She feels pleasantly surprised when her kids beat her in board games, enthusiastic toward unexpected adventures, and overwhelmed by the generosity of God.